"And yet surely to alchemy this right is due, that it may be compared to the husbandman whereof Aesop makes the fable, that when he died he told his sons that he had left unto them gold buried under the ground in his vineyard: and they digged over the ground, gold they found none, but by reason of their stirring and digging the mould about the roots of their vines, they had a great vintage the year following: so assuredly the search and stir to make gold hath brought to light a great number of good and fruitful inventions and experiments, as well for the disclosing of nature as for the use of man's life."
— Francis Bacon, *The Advancement Of Learning*

Revised 4/2015: Minor formatting changes

CreateSpace, Charleston SC

ISBN-13: 978-1505677324
ISBN-10: 1505677327

Book Cover: Laura LaBrun Hatcher, laura@hatcherdesignoffice.com

Legal Disclaimer

The author has attempted to provide a balanced approach and understanding of topics discussed in this book. However, any use of information provided is entirely at the reader's discretion. The reader should consult with their health care practitioner before engaging in any new dietary, herbal or nutritional therapies. Additionally, the reader should consult with their doctor before stopping any current medications or therapies. This information is not intended to replace or be a substitute for psychological counseling or therapy, but rather to augment and support them.

Special Thanks

I am immensely grateful for the generous support of those who assisted me during various stages of writing this book. I would like to thank my wonderful husband, Richard, for his faith in me, his support on my journey and his staunch love. I am grateful to my sons, Mark, Jonathan and Nick, who have helped me continue to grow and challenge my assumptions and worldviews. Thanks to Randall and Elizabeth Holm for believing in me even when I had stopped believing in myself, and for holding my feet to the fire in the most loving and kind ways when I needed it. I'm grateful to Michael J. Rizzolo for his example of the power of alchemy. I am humbled by the love, skill and attention that went into reading and editing by Melissa Peet. Heartfelt thanks to Susan Johnson-Smith for coordinating all aspects involved in the book design. Deep gratitude to Laura LeBrun Hatcher for creating and giving me such a beautiful book cover. I could not have written this book without the support, love and examples of all these people. Thank you all.

The Art of Personal Alchemy

Transform Your Emotional Lead into Gold

Dr. Diane Gross

Table of Contents

Preface

Alchemy is an ancient idea that suggests that one can transform base, worthless metals into gold or silver via a secret and mystical process. The ability to do this was purported to demonstrate profound powers. But the principle of alchemy is not limited to transforming metals. It can also be applied to emotional growth and transformation. Alchemy of this kind includes transforming painful and negative experiences into positive outcomes. It comes by learning to master your thoughts, your attitudes and your energy.

Imagine that I am holding a raw egg in my hand. The shell is fragile, yet paradoxically, incredibly strong. I can squeeze the egg with a lot of force, but as long as the pressure is even on all sides, it will not break. However, if I apply just a bit of focused pressure with my thumb, the eggshell fractures. If I smash and grind it in my hand, it breaks into a thousand pieces.

The egg is a good metaphor for life. If there is a balanced, healthy environment, we can take a lot of pressure without breaking. But if specific pressure is applied without consideration and attention to balance, then there may be damage. If there is significant abuse, a life can seem shattered.

What do you do if you feel your life has been damaged or shattered? How do you repair the injury to your psyche and emotions? Or is it even possible? The answer is a resounding YES! You will never be the same as before the damaging experience, just as an egg can never be put back together. But you can evolve into a more mature, more resilient and wiser you. It is what you *do* with each experience that makes the difference. Take a look at the picture below.* It is made completely of eggshells. This is what each of us has the opportunity to do with the pieces of our lives. What makes this possible is the art of personal alchemy. It's the process of transforming emotional lead into gold.

Photo by Diane Gross

Another metaphor for using painful experiences to transform emotional lead into gold is a type of pottery from Japan called Kintsukuroi.* Kintsukuroi means "to repair with gold". It is the art of repairing broken or cracked pottery with gold or silver lacquer. The message is that the piece is more beautiful for having been broken.

Photos by Lakesidepottery: Tea bowl repair using kintsugi (or Kintsukuroi.) thrown and repaired by Morty Bachar, Lakeside Pottery www.lakesidepottery.com

In some poorer countries where there is a scarcity of wood, visitors sometimes are greeted by a strange sight - round, petrifying manure patties laid out on rocks. Residents have gathered the excrement of the local animals and formed them into disks to dry in the sun. After they are dried, the manure patties are burned for fuel and cooking. These societies take something that most of us would find distinctly objectionable and use in a way that greatly enhances their lives. We all have some measure of 'crap' in our lives. If we transform those experiences into something useful, we too can change our lives for the better.

I tell my story here briefly, not to elicit sympathy, but rather to share the power of alchemy in my own life. I hold no illusion that my childhood is in any way unique. Certainly I had moments of fun and play, but the backdrop was one of uncertainty, insecurity and fear.

We moved a lot when I was growing up. I was constantly the 'new kid', and developed a belief of that I didn't belong. This affected every relationship I had for many years. I was perpetually insecure and afraid that people wouldn't like or accept me. Most of the men in my life as a child were abusive. One time my school called the police because I had so many bruises on my body. One step-father was sexually abusive. I developed a paradigm that people in authority are not to be trusted because they will hurt me. I came to believe I deserved to be abused.

As a young woman I struggled with anorexia and obsessive compulsive disorder. At one point I was also diagnosed with fibromyalgia and chronic fatigue syndrome. My back was in a state of chronic spasm. It felt as if my life and world were falling apart and completely out of my control. My emotional pain was manifesting in severe psychological and physical agony.

Many of the things I came to believe about myself and life in general caused me to experience profound suffering and prevented me from living from a place of joy and healing. Emotional pain is often rooted in what we were taught and how we were treated as children. I eventually realized that what I had come to believe as a child no longer served me. I decided it was my responsibility and my right to change those beliefs into ones that were empowering and productive. The lens through which experiences are filtered can be changed, but it requires making deliberate choices.

That is what this book is about. This book shares my alchemic process and illuminates my personal paradigm. I hope it assists and blesses you on your path.

*The eggshell and kintsukuroi images can be seen in full color at
www.theartofpersonalalchemy.com

Chapter 1

Paradigms

"We don't see things as they are, we see them as we are." Anaïs Nin

"We live in a world that worships limitations." Tama Kieves.

How you view yourself, your world and your experiences profoundly impacts your emotions and sense of well-being. In the same way in which different colored glasses impact how you see things, so too your paradigms act as filters that impact your perceptions and experiences. Webster defines paradigm broadly as: "a philosophical or theoretical framework of any kind." So a paradigm serves as a framework within which ideas, theories, perspectives and generalizations are formed. If the paradigm changes, then too those theories, perspectives and generalizations must change - just as changing your pair of colored glasses changes the view.

Your paradigms can help you realize happiness, acceptance and joy in your life; or pain, resistance and suffering. This book is intended to provide assistance in changing your paradigms to ones that create the kind of life and experiences for which you yearn. Paradigms can change. You can change the ones that are creating turmoil in your life. How do I know? I have done it throughout my adult life in both small and large ways.

Choosing helpful paradigms is an essential aspect of the emotional alchemic process. There are empowering and helpful paradigms, as well as disempowering and pain producing paradigms. All paradigms do not have an equal effect on your emotions and life. One paradigm might be extremely empowering or disempowering, and another empowering or disempowering to a lesser degree. Those that are the most disempowering will create the most pain, while the most empowering will create the most joy.

Sometimes people mistake an empowering paradigm for a Pollyanna, "pie in the sky" way of viewing the world. But it's not about denying the reality of a situation. Seeing the potential benefit in any given situation is not denial. It is not about looking the other way, or covering your ears and eyes, refusing to see the facts. To do so is actually disempowering because it removes your ability to respond in a pro-active and meaningful way. If a person comes to a doctor with a broken leg, it is not helpful to focus on the unbroken leg while ignoring the broken one. If a tire on your car is flat, it is not wise to ignore it, encouraging yourself with the thought that you at least have three well-inflated tires. A paradigm shift involves completely accepting the reality of the situation, yet viewing it in such a way that is heartening and elevating.

An empowered paradigm is also not about living a pain-free life. Pain does not mean that you are a failure. We all experience pain at different points in our lives. An empowering paradigm allows you to find ways to still find hope, joy and possible benefit in the midst of the pain.

Most people can recall an experience that at the time seemed quite negative, yet turned out to be profoundly positive. Years ago, a few weeks before I graduated from a school of Oriental Medicine, it looked like my husband was going to be laid off. I was not working at the time, and the prospect of both of us being without an income sent me into a tailspin. Actually, I was terrified! I cried for days. Since where we lived had a high saturation of Doctors of Oriental Medicine, I would no longer have the luxury of leisurely building my practice after graduation. I ended up accepting a job out of state. As it turned out my husband's job was to end five months after my job began. I moved across the country alone, with him scheduled to join me later.

I had never had my own room, much less lived alone. And there I was on the other side of the country, in a strange city, in a new apartment…alone. The first night I went to the nearest department store to buy a television set so I wouldn't feel so lonely. One of the first things I heard was a news report about a man who was breaking into single women's apartments and raping them. Due to sexual abuse I experienced as a child, I still carried a strong sense of vulnerability in that area. For five months I had the opportunity to squarely face, and let go of, my fear. It wasn't a fun experience, but it was an extremely beneficial one for my own emotional healing.

Over time I found I enjoyed living in our new city much more than the previous one. When my husband joined me, he was offered a job in a field that he had been trying to enter for years. A few years later our granddaughter was born. In our new residence we lived close enough to see her far more frequently than if we had not moved. An event that I had initially labeled 'negative' turned out to be one of the biggest blessings of our lives. It was a powerful lesson.

People often stay in disempowering paradigms because of the emotional payoffs. Some common ones are receiving attention, a ready excuse for failure and a reprieve from accountability. I remember coming home from work one day, feeling really good. When I walked in the house my husband asked "How are you feeling?" I responded with, "Well, I'm pretty tired." Then I laughed at myself. I guess I believed whoever was the most tired didn't have to make dinner. I realized I had played the victim. I decided to never do that again. From then on if my husband asked me that question and I didn't want to make dinner I replied with, "I feel fine, but I don't want to make dinner tonight." That felt like a much healthier way to get my need to have a relaxing evening without the obligation to make dinner met.

Developing empowering paradigms is something we all can choose to do. In general it doesn't happen by accident. It can be helpful to employ some strategies to consciously make paradigm shifts in areas of your life where you feel stuck. The strategies outlined in this book are ones I have personally used in my life and found extremely helpful. I have also had the honor of teaching and coaching others in using these approaches. In my personal experience, choosing more empowering paradigms simply makes life more enjoyable.

Chapter 2

Personal Responsibility

"Life is not a matter of having good cards, but of playing a poor hand well."
- Robert Louis Stevenson

"The search for a scapegoat is the easiest of all hunting expeditions."
Dwight D. Eisenhower

Taking responsibility for your life doesn't mean that you are to blame for growing up in an abusive home environment, or for any later mistreatment you may have experienced. It means making a choice to use each experience to learn, grow, and become more loving and mature. It means you are willing to take responsibility from this moment forward for how you respond to whatever circumstances, experiences and events you encounter.

We live in a culture that promotes victimhood. But blaming someone, or life circumstance, for your current unhappiness can keep you stuck in painful paradigms. Change cannot occur until you take responsibility for your choices and your life. Choosing to accept responsibility for your own life makes space for hope. If you believe you cannot be happy or successful unless someone or something else changes, then you are in effect a hostage. However, if you decide to forge your own path, then there is hope for transformation; the power belongs to you rather than something or someone outside of you.

Sometimes people equate taking personal responsibility for their lives with letting those they feel mistreated them off the hook. It is possible, however, to hold people accountable for unacceptable behavior and still choose to respond in responsible and empowering ways. Two of my stepfathers did abuse me. It was wrong and deeply hurtful. I don't condone, excuse or minimize it. I think each of them should be accountable for their behavior. That accountability may be legal and/or moral. I do, however, refuse to allow my stepfathers' abuse to define me or to dictate my behavior for the rest of my life.

It is not helpful to blame your current life on circumstances. Each person must take responsibility for their own life. Blame looks to the past. Taking responsibility lives in the present. Blame is disempowering. Blame says "I'm this way because…" Responsibility says "This happened to me. What can I do now to heal and live with joy?" Taking responsibility is empowering. Blame looks for fault. Taking responsibility for your own life demonstrates a commitment to improving, healing, and growing.

It isn't unusual for people to want their lives to be different, without actually making any internal or personal changes. But any empowering life transformation requires personal choice and action. As Leo Tolstoy once said "Everyone thinks of changing the world, but no one thinks of changing himself".

In her book "The Happiness Habit", Pam Golen shared the results of an interview with two brothers. One was a multi-millionaire and the other a homeless alcoholic. The brothers grew up in an extremely toxic home environment with alcoholic parents. Interestingly, each brother felt their current life circumstance was a direct result of growing up in their dysfunctional home. The rich brother described the experience as the motivating factor in his desire to do something better and succeed. The homeless brother designated it as the reason for his downfall. Each assigned his own meaning to his experience.

To take personal responsibility you also have to move away from co-dependence. Co-dependence involves taking responsibility for other people's choices, and sacrificing your own well-being in order to please them. Living co-dependently is living in a state of fear. It is seeking to satisfy the perceived needs of someone else in order to gain acceptance. Co-dependence limits your ability to hear your own inner voice of wisdom and to make the choices and paradigm shifts that will inspire your life and bring you joy. Shifting into a paradigm of personal responsibility suggests that each person is accountable for their own choices, responses and lives. That doesn't negate the fact that we are also all inter-dependent. We live in relationship with ourselves, with our friends and family, with our local communities and with the global community. Recognize the difference, however, between acknowledging and respecting how our choices and actions impact one another, and seeking to mold your life around someone else to the exclusion on your own needs and desires.

In order to accept personal responsibility for the course of your life, you must be aware that you have choices and what those choices are. If you are unaware that you *have* a choice, it is impossible to select a different approach or path. You are simply in default mode. The challenge is that you may not know what it is that you don't know. In other words, you may not currently have insight into healthier more empowered ways to approach a situation. You may feel stuck, but can't see a way out. This is one reason it is important to make time to seek out and learn about ways to develop yourself. Reading, listening to CDs on self-growth, watching DVDs discussing personal growth topics, attending workshops and seminars, meditating, and associating with groups and individuals who are dedicated to personal evolution can all be wonderful ways to help you learn healthier and more empowering ways to deal with your life challenges.

As we grow from childhood to adulthood we all are taught, and adopt, certain perspectives and beliefs about ourselves and the world around us. But beliefs are just a habitual way of thinking within your current paradigm. If current beliefs do not serve you, or make you happy, you can change them into ones that do. Any habit, including a habitual way of thinking, can be changed. It may take a bit of time and focus, but it is possible.

When changing a habit it often takes more energy to get started than to keep going. A good analogy is launching a rocket into space. The vast majority of the fuel required to send a rocket to the moon is used up in the first few minutes as the rocket gathers the speed and force necessary to escape the gravitational pull of the earth. Once that has been accomplished, very little fuel is required to keep it going. One vital aspect of personal responsibility is that of framing your experiences in the most helpful and mature way possible, because the meaning you give your experiences makes an enormous difference in the quality of your emotional life. This topic will be addressed in more detail in the chapter on Empowered Emotions. It is important to remember that choosing to view your experiences from a more comprehensive, inclusive perspective allows you to respond intentionally to events in your life rather than merely react to them.

Personal responsibility allows you to recognize that no past situation need determine your potential for success in life. It recognizes and acknowledges your past within a larger context; understands that your life is much more than your history. It allows you to unwrap the gifts that may have been overlooked in what you have gone through. It is a purposeful decision to not allow your life to be hijacked by your past or current suffering, but rather to acknowledge your power to choose something different. Some people who have come from the direst situations have achieved great things - not in spite of, but because of, what they learned from their experience. It can be convenient, even easy, to use the past as an excuse, but each of us has the power to choose to rise above events in our past and realize our true potential. It may not always be easy, but it is always worth the investment of time and energy.

We are taught that if we grow up in an unhealthy or hurtful environment, it means we are irreparably damaged. I actually have heard psychologists, parents and teachers say a child will be "scarred for life" because of something they experienced. I've even heard this said in the presence of the abused child. What a hopeless paradigm. The message the child received is that they were broken and had no chance at a joyful and fulfilled life! Disempowering, to say the least.

There is a new and long-needed branch of psychology surfacing in the field of mental health: Positive Psychology. It is based on the idea that painful experiences do not create exclusively negative results; much deepening and strengthening can result as well. Since the inception of modern day psychology, treatment has focused almost exclusively on pain. This approach has done a lot of damage, in part because what we focus tends to grow and expand.

There can be definite advantages to difficult experiences, including that of a tough childhood. In the book "Cradles of Eminence" by Victor Goertzel, Mildred Goertzel, Ted Goertzel and Ariel M.W. Hansen, the authors discuss over 700 famous and successful people in history who seemed to succeed not in spite of, but rather *because of,* their adversities. A scientific principle called the Adversity Principle asserts that lack of challenges yields only a small measure of growth and strengthening. The unprotected tree in the forest clearing that endures the most buffeting from the wind and elements tends to be much healthier and stronger than the one protected on all sides by other trees. Breaking the eggshell for a chick instead of letting it struggle can seriously compromise its ability to survive. Helping a butterfly escape from its chrysalis may spell its death, as is exemplified in this story.

The Butterfly

A man found a butterfly cocoon. He watched the cocoon for several days. One day a tiny opening appeared in the cocoon. He sat very still and watched as the butterfly struggled for several hours to force itself through the tiny hole of its cocoon. Then it seemed to stop making progress. It appeared to the man as if the butterfly had gone as far as it could, and could go no further, so he decided to help the butterfly out of the cocoon.

He snipped the remaining bit of the cocoon with scissors, and the butterfly emerged effortlessly. There was something strange, however. The butterfly had a swollen body, and its wings were shriveled. The man watched closely, expecting that the wings would enlarge and expand to support the body, which would contract in time. Neither

17

happened. In fact, the butterfly spent the rest of its short life crawling around with a swollen body and deformed wings. It was never able to fly.

Though the man acted in kindness, what he didn't understand was that the restricting cocoon and the struggle required for the butterfly to get through the small opening of the cocoon were critical pieces of the process of forcing fluid from the body of the butterfly into its wings so that it would be ready to fly once it has achieved its freedom from the cocoon.   Author Unknown

I certainly am not implying that we should seek out pain, or that we should purposely inflict it on others in some twisted rationale that we are somehow helping people to grow. We all have a right to be loved and treated with kindness, and we all have a need to love and treat others kindly. To act in opposition to that goes against our deepest, most intrinsic spiritual nature. What I am suggesting is that when we experience the inevitable hardships in life, those experiences can be utilized to help break open our hearts, to make us stronger and more resilient, and to cause us to grow in meaningful ways.

You are the only one who can live your life. If you are not happy with it, then it is up to you to find a way to change it. It is your responsibility to learn what you need to do to improve your life and make a paradigm shift. If you don't change, your life won't change.

Chapter 3

Empowered Thinking

"Confidence comes not from always being right but from not fearing to be wrong." Peter T McIntyre

"Freedom is what you do with what's been done to you." John Paul Sartre

Recent studies in neurobiology reveal a strong connection between thought and emotion.[1] Sometimes people miss this vital aspect of cultivating a healthy emotional life. Specific thoughts have the power to generate corresponding emotional states. Sad thoughts generate sad feelings. Frustrated thoughts create feelings of frustration, etc. Often the specific thought is habituated and occurs so quickly that it is unnoticed. If someone came up to you and slapped you in the face, you might experience instant anger, but reflection and self-inquiry will reveal an anger triggering thought. The thought might be, "how dare you hit me. You have no right!" Conversely, if you had an underlying thought that the strike was deserved or justified, there would be no rise of anger, but rather acceptance. There is always a relationship between thought and emotional experience. The way you feel is generally a reflection of your underlying beliefs and thoughts.

Because emotions are often precipitated by what you think, it can be useful develop awareness of what you are thinking, and to identify habitual thought patterns. You can then begin to nurture those that encourage positive and empowered emotions. It can be useful to spend a few days observing, and maybe even writing down, every thought that comes into your mind. This practice can help you begin to see what your 'thought life' is like. It will also provide some clarity about your emotional life. I remember feeling shocked when I did this for the first time. When I reviewed my notes at the end of the day I was struck by how negative most of the thoughts had been. What was also interesting is that it had felt like a particularly good day. It was a revelatory moment.

As children we all learn and absorb thoughts, beliefs and perspectives from loved ones, authority figures, peers, and media. Some of the information and messages you received may have been helpful, and some of it decidedly not. Some of the ideas we adopt as our own are simply unquestioned beliefs and concepts that have been passed down from one generation to another. Some of these may even be the residual of societal expectations and norms that are no longer relevant to our time.

Many of our thoughts and beliefs have been birthed out of pain and fear-based responses from others that we observed, or of which we were casualties. We assigned personal meaning to things that were said or done to us that were hurtful. Most of the thoughts you habitually and automatically think were learned and adopted when you were a child. These habituated thoughts form your beliefs. As a child you simply accepted whatever you were taught as true, since the information came from adults and authority figures. But thoughts are essentially neurons that are firing in the brain. A belief is developed over time by thoughts that repeatedly fire until they become the dominant thought. Belief is simply habitual thought.

Thought patterns acquired during childhood become your default unless you make an intentional shift. Sometimes the thought constructs you learned as a child no longer fit. They may not be true for you, but you may still act as if they are. It can be helpful to review your current belief systems, and decide which ones still serve you and which ones do not. Once you have identified which beliefs you no longer want to embrace, steps can then be taken to release them and form new ones that are better aligned with who you want to be.

Some beliefs formed in childhood may be obvious and easy to discharge as an adult. For example, I was taught as a child that if you break a mirror you will have seven years of bad luck. As an adult it was fairly easy for me to identify this as a thought or belief that I didn't want to keep. I choose to believe that breaking a mirror has no bearing on my future luck. I choose to believe that I create my own future based on the choices I make and the level of integrity with which I live my life. Some beliefs, however, are pivotal, more insidious and more impactful. For example, I grew up with the habituated thought and belief that men are never around – and if they are, they hurt you! When I revisited that belief as an adult I decided it was an unfair and prejudicial position. I did some work to release that belief and instill one that better represented what I believed was more accurate. I now choose to believe that men are individuals just like women. Some actively seek kindness, some do not. Some live out of their own pain, and some live from a more loving place. Some value honesty, some do not.

Our thoughts and beliefs inform our assumptions. Assumptions are based on unquestioned beliefs about how things and people do, or should, function. Assumptions feed and are fed by our thoughts and paradigms. If, for example, I assume that all men are like my stepfathers were, then that is going to affect every relationship I have with men – including with my husband and sons.

Our thoughts, beliefs and assumptions also dictate our level of success. Roger Bannister is a perfect example of this. It had always been thought that a four minute mile was impossible. It was believed to be outside the parameters of human capacity. In 1954 Roger Bannister broke the four minute mile. The world was stunned. After he broke that barrier people no longer thought it was impossible. His record was broken numerous times during the following year, and that time is now considered well within reach. Your belief about what you can and cannot do often dictates your ability to do it.

There are practices I have found useful for shifting into more empowering ways of thinking. Some of them may take time to effect a discernible change, while others may result in more immediate shifts in perspective. Each is potent.

Recognize That Stress is Internal: The word 'stress' is not a helpful construct. It implies something external is happening which automatically elicits stressful feelings. However, stress is not 'out there'. Stress is not a thing. It is an internal response based on your perception and interpretation of what is occurring. I much prefer the word 'trigger' to 'stress' because it acknowledges that something *is* happening that is triggering within you something that is *already* there. Sometimes this is an old emotional wound or an unresolved issue, but the emotional 'button' is being pushed by the situation. Later in the book I will discuss strategies that will help you recognize and process these emotional triggers.

Affirm Truth: It is helpful to affirm what is true on a daily basis rather than simply succumbing to habituated negative self-talk. Affirming the truth of your potential is an essential aspect of deliberately putting into your mind the thoughts that you want to become your natural default. In order for a thought to become a habitual pattern, it must be thought frequently and consistently. It's important to remember that developing new thought patterns is a process. Accepting that it will take time will make it a much easier and more graceful route. Planting an acorn and expecting a tree to grow overnight would be frustrating and disappointing. When a seed is planted, nourished and weeded, it will naturally grow. So too, thoughts need time to take root and grow. They also need to be nourished, and old thoughts weeded out in order to optimize results. Just as surely as an oak tree will grow from an acorn with adequate time, so too will a new thought life grow when you plant the appropriate seeds.

An effective way to nurture helpful thoughts on a daily basis is through the use of affirmations. This practice has been dismissed as ineffective by some who have unsuccessfully tried using daily affirmations. Lack of success is often due to the omission of some essential components of a successful affirmation, along with feeling disingenuous when an affirmation doesn't feel truthful. Self-honesty is vital to personal, emotional and spiritual growth. Attempting to fake your way into a higher level of consciousness can create tremendous internal conflict. Tiered-believability affirmations, as discussed in chapter 5, resolve both of these issues. They allow you to move toward your desired goal with complete authenticity and honesty.

Another aspect of affirming what is true is to challenge what is untrue. Don't let statements such as, "I'm so stupid!" roll off your tongue unchallenged. Stop yourself immediately and declare the truth! "No, I'm not stupid at all. I made a mistake and now I'm going to focus on what I need to do to move forward". Self-correct whenever it comes into your awareness that you are speaking or thinking things that you don't want as part of your experience.

Reframing: Our experience of life is always an outgrowth of our internal life. The way in which we interpret the outer world, and the meaning which we assign to events, determines the quality of our life. Reframing means making a deliberate decision about how you are going to view an experience.

How you experience your life is determined by the meaning you give to the things that happen. It's a powerful way in which to reduce feelings of stress, as well as create more joy in your life. For example, if you were laid off, you might view it as an opportunity to explore another line of work that would be more fulfilling rather than as a devastating blow to your career. If you missed your plane you could decide it is an opportunity to buy a good book and simply relax. A traffic jam can bring the gift of time – to take a breath... Standing in a long line at the grocery store at the end of a long day of work can be viewed as an opportunity to develop your capacity for patience and broaden your perspective on what really matters. A time of illness can be framed as an opening for reassessing and evaluating priorities and life-style choices.

Reframing means making a choice to find the best possible context in which to see and interpret your experience. It is not about denying what is happening. It is about finding and optimizing the unnoticed potential good in the situation.

Start Where You Are: You must start exactly where you are. You cannot start where you are not. The potential for change lies dormant until you recognize and accept your current state. You can only grow from where you are. It is important to see the reality of where your choices have brought you, as well as the potential for change. See things for what they are, as well as what they can be. The glass is not half full *or* half empty – it is half full *and* half empty. When you accept that, then you have a choice of whether to start filling your glass further or drink what's there. When you have moved out of a state of denial, then you can authentically explore the inherent potential for change. With awareness comes the ability to choose.

Stop Limiting Yourself: I want to tell you a secret. I'm not meant to own a toaster. It's just not in the cards for me. I know it is fine for some people, but I've always known that having a toaster was not part of my destiny. It's not something God wants for me. Ever.

Does that sound slightly ridiculous to you? Yet this is the same rationale many people use for why they don't allow themselves to want or enjoy certain things in life. "I'm not meant to be financially well off." "Finding a meaningful relationship just isn't in the cards for me." "Having a job I like just isn't in God's plans for me." And on it goes…

Most limitations are self-imposed. The truth is that you are meant to enjoy all of the blessings and abundance that life has to offer. If there is something that you would truly enjoy, don't limit yourself by telling yourself you aren't meant to have it. If you want it, are willing to dedicate the time, work and energy to achieve it – then start now to move in the direction of your desire.

Be a Gatekeeper for Your Subconscious: Your conscious mind is the gatekeeper for your subconscious. This is critical because your subconscious is what actually determines and stores your beliefs and habituated mental and emotional responses. It essentially runs your life. Your subconscious has no filter, it simply accepts whatever input it receives as truth. Even more, it doesn't know the difference between what is real and what is not real. It's why you can awaken from a frightening dream dripping with sweat and heart pounding. Your subconscious didn't know it wasn't real. It's why, if you close your eyes and vividly imagine a tarantula starting to crawl up your leg, you start to feel a strong urge to escape. It's why imaging the taste and smell of chocolate cake can make you salivate.

Though your conscious mind is able to differentiate between reality and fantasy when you are watching a violent movie, your subconscious takes it all in. Over time your subconscious mind becomes programmed to view the world as a violent and fearful place. Watching commercials, movies and television programs and books that focus on sickness and ill health conditions us to subconsciously accept and incorporate sickness into our lives. Whatever we allow into our awareness and experience, our subconscious mind accepts as true - even if on a conscious level we know it is simply fantasy.

Research in neuro-plasticity, the ability of the brain to change and adapt itself, has demonstrated that images and/or sounds can cause instant and measureable chemical and neurological changes.[1] Pleasant images and sounds elicit changes that help support feelings of well-being and contentment. Disturbing images and sounds create changes in the brain and body that lead to feelings of distress and uneasiness.

Even if your subconscious mind could understand that what it is seeing or experiencing is not real, your brain is still being entrained. Entrainment occurs when the energy, or vibration, of one thing influences and changes the energy of something or someone else. For example, if you hold two tuning forks side by side, striking one of them on the edge of the table, causing it to vibrate, it will soon cause the other fork to vibrate. This happens because the first fork is entraining the second to resonate at the same vibration.

Current research in the field of quantum physics has demonstrated that everything in the universe vibrates.[2] That includes you. Every molecule and atom in your body is vibrating. Further, it has been found that whatever you bring into your environment impacts your personal vibration. Emotions affect and are affected by your vibration. Images and sounds of anger, fear, sadness, etc. entrain your energy to adapt patterns that resonate with those emotions. What you watch, listen to, read and are close to can impact your personal vibration.

Be Open to Change: There is a famous story of a man who was sent to see a psychiatrist because he was convinced he was dead. The psychiatrist tried numerous ways to help the man see that he was, in fact, very much alive. Finally he hit on a plan. He asked the man if dead people could bleed. The man responded that dead people could not bleed. The psychiatrist asked him to prove he was dead by pricking his thumb. If he was dead, then he shouldn't bleed. The man consented and pricked his thumb, which, of course, bled. His response? "Well, what do you know! Dead people *do* bleed!"

Your beliefs drive your perceptions. If you have already decided what is true and what isn't, then you will interpret your experiences through the filter of that belief. It can be helpful to become aware of what underlying beliefs and assumptions inform your life view. Additionally, entertaining the possibility that *you could be mistaken* can provide an opening for positive change should more information present itself.

Identify Unhelpful Thoughts: Learn to identify the thoughts and beliefs that help support what you want to create in your life, and those that do not support your desired outcome. It can be instructive to illuminate your automatic, habituated thoughts. One activity that can help is to write each word below on the top of a separate sheet of paper. You should have 8 sheets of paper. On each page write every thought that comes into your head as you think about your relationship with each topic. Give yourself plenty of time. It is better to do one page per day and take your time than to do all categories in a hurried manner.

Some examples of habituated thoughts might be, "I have too much work to do." "I hate my job." "I love what I do." "I have no friends." "I am so lucky." "If people really knew me they wouldn't like me." "Money doesn't grow on trees." "She is such a headache." "There is never enough time." "I'm always given what I need." "God is gonna get me." "I never get what I want."…etc. This will help distill, crystallize and clarify what your underlying thoughts and beliefs are about each topic.

> Work
> Relationships
> Money
> Spiritual
> Leisure/play
> Success

Wait for the Harvest: It's important to keep in mind that it can take some time for the seeds you are planting in your mind and life to grow. Robert Louis Stevenson once said, "Don't judge each day by the harvest you reap, but by the seeds that you plant." His point is well taken. It would be unrealistic to expect a field full of corn ready to be harvested tomorrow if you only sowed the corn seed today. Growth takes time. That is the nature of life.

If you sow that which you want to reap; if you do the work of watering, weeding and nourishing the seeds, they will, in due course, grow into a bountiful crop. So too with the "thought seeds" you plant, water and nourish. In the words of a Chinese proverb, "All of the flowers of all the tomorrows lie in the seeds of today".

Chapter 4

Authentic Emotions

"You can't change the fruit without changing the root." Stephen Covey

"And the day came when the risk to remain tight in a bud was more painful than the risk it took to blossom." Anaïs Nin

I don't elect to use the word 'stress.' It implies that the source of the discomfort being experienced has primarily an external source. In my private practice as a Doctor of Oriental Medicine I specialize in the treatment of psycho-emotional concerns. Frequently patients ask me to treat them for stress. When I ask them what they are feeling stressful about, often the reply is, "My work is stressful." But if it was their work that was stressful, then everyone who ever did that work would experience stress, which is highly unlikely. It's how you think about a situation that produces the feelings of stress. I prefer the word 'trigger' to the word 'stress'. The word 'trigger' acknowledges that something is occurring outside of you, but that the source of the stressful response is internal. It recognizes that your emotional sensitivities are evidence of an emotional wound beneath the reaction. If you live with the paradigm that stress happens to you, rather than within you, then you will always be like a leaf at the mercy of the wind.

Stress is not external. It is an internal experience, and you take your internal experiences wherever you go. That's the reason that no matter where you go, or what external changes take place, generally your internal emotional state quickly returns to the same baseline. Chronic feelings of stress can be a cue that you may have some paradigms that are creating pain. Sometimes this is a result of basic belief systems, thought patterns and coping strategies that need to be updated. It can also be indicative of a need to make a shift in some of the neuro-physical and energetic patterns and pathways that have developed over time. The way thoughts and emotions become established and habitual is much like a rivulet that begins carving out a small rut in the earth on a hill during a rainstorm. The first rain may cause a very small groove in the earth, but each subsequent rainstorm increasingly deepens that groove. Thoughts and emotions also travel along certain neuro-pathways. The more frequently you have a specific thought or emotion, the more established the neuro-pathway for that thought or emotion becomes. This is the way in which your body and brain retains information and experiences so that you don't have to relearn each time. Ways of thinking and emotional reactions become habituated in this way. These pathways can be altered if a change occurs. Current research in brain studies have demonstrated that people can intentionally change the neuro-pathways in their bodies utilizing certain techniques.[3]

The primary way to begin to heal emotional wounds is to recognize that emotional discomfort and pain are cues that healing needs to occur. Emotional healing starts with asking the question, "What is being triggered within me that is causing me to experience this pain?" Then work on healing that.

A core disempowering paradigm is an external locus of control. An external locus of control means approaching life as if it happens *to* you. An internal locus of control acknowledges that your personal choices determine how you experience life. An external locus of control can contribute to emotional distress and pain. An internal locus of control fosters feelings of peace and confidence.

While most of us are not yet evolved enough to create every desired experience, we can certainly make choices about how we respond to life situations. Nick Vujicic is someone who understands and lives this principle. Nick was born without any arms or legs. There was no apparent reason that the doctors could point to. Many in Nick's situation might have lived life from an external locus of control. They might have chosen to engage in self-pity and viewed themselves as a victim of circumstance. Nick chose to come at life from an internal locus of control and embrace his life. He is an amazing example of someone who deeply loves life, exudes joy and finds opportunity in every experience. He travels around the world speaking to people about the transformational power of choosing your own attitude.

In order to regularly experience peace, joy and health, it is essential to have an internal locus of control. An internal locus of control doesn't ask "Why is this happening to me?", but instead, "What can I do to create change?" An external locus of control keeps you stuck; while an internal one helps you find empowering choices.

Once, during a workshop, someone made the point that there are times when an external locus of control is meaningful, surrendering a situation over which you truly have no control to God, or a higher power. I think that is true, but I would submit that making the decision to turn the situation over is also a choice. So the choice to surrender can also be a type of internal locus of control. In those types of situations, we can do something about it. We can let it go and ask for help.

As a practitioner of Oriental Medicine I have the privilege of assisting people with balancing their emotions. The most common painful emotions I see people struggling with are anger (the full continuum includes frustration, irritation, rage, etc.), fear (including worry, anxiety, tension, feeling stressed, etc.), and sadness (including depression, emotional lethargy, feeling numb, etc.).

Everyone experiences painful emotions from time to time; the difficulty arises when emotional distress becomes chronic. There may be a variety of reasons why otherwise transient emotional discomfort becomes protracted. Nutritional deficiencies, chemical imbalances, learned coping behaviors, low emotional IQ and unresolved emotional trauma may all play a part in long-standing stressful emotions.

If you experience lingering stressful emotions, those patterns can become habituated in the body on a neuro-chemical and physiological level. In other words, emotions are frequently habits! So if you experience chronic fear, or sadness, or other stressful feelings, you have gotten into an emotional habit. The good news is that any habit can be unlearned. These patterns can be changed, but it does require intention and strategic intervention.

Emotional turmoil is sometimes part of growth. Even in nature, according to chaos theory, systems typically deconstruct in order to reorganize at a higher, more efficient level. Discomfort, especially chronic discomfort, can be a signal that you need to make some changes. People sometimes become used to, and even comfortable, in their current situations and thus resist change. It is sometimes easier to remain the same than to take the risk of transforming your life in yet unknown ways.

Utilizing personal alchemy principles can be a powerful way in which to *use* painful emotions for personal growth and transformation. As I mentioned earlier, I use the word 'trigger' when an event sparks a strong emotional reaction. Recognizing this, and getting to the root of the emotional reaction, can be an effective vehicle for personal, emotional and spiritual evolution. Using painful emotions as markers to help you understand where you still need internal healing allows you to accept your current experience, release it and then move beyond it. This process can help you respond to an event from an empowered paradigm rather than react from a place of emotional pain.

You may often have more choice about your emotions than you realize. Abraham Lincoln said, "People are just about as happy as they make up their minds to be." While I do think this is a simplistic approach to the topic of emotions and choice, I think the idea of making choices about one's emotional experience is a topic worth discussing. While clinical depression and other severe physiological and chemical imbalances must be given special consideration, many experiences of emotional discomfort can be shifted with a change in perspective and choice. Exercising this choice is key to personal alchemy.

I remember once, years ago, going to work in a bad mood. I felt irritable, cranky and frustrated. I struggled through the entire morning in this frame of mind. Later in the day I asked my boss, who I had never seen in an irritated state, "How do you get out of a bad mood?" He asked me an illuminating question. "If I gave you one million dollars right now, but only on the proviso that you had to immediately change into a happy, positive mood – and I could see inside of you and know if you had done it or not – could you do it?" My immediate response was, "Of course!" He then said, "Then it isn't really a matter of whether you can do it or not, it's just if you want to badly enough." That stopped me in my tracks. I realized in that moment that if the payoff was strong enough I could do it. It was within my power. I had to choose whether or not I was willing to put in the effort to do it.

Are there times when your emotions may be too strong or entrenched to change with a simple mental choice? I think there are times when that is the case. Emotions are a physiological, or full-body, experience. You may have a pharmacopeia of chemicals and hormones surging through your body due to a sub-conscious reaction to an event. Your blood may rush from your brain's reasoning centers to the emotional centers, making it difficult to even think straight. Logic alone will not suffice during these times. You can't talk yourself out of feeling terrified, for example, if your body is flooded with adrenaline and your emotional brain has taken the reins. There are things, however, that you can do to immediately start moving toward greater emotional balance.

You can improve your emotional health by choosing empowered ways in which to express your emotions. This is the essential difference between reacting and responding. Reacting is reflexive, and lacks the element of personal power and choice. Responding is the conscious use of empowered choice. Victor Frankl, psychiatrist and author of "Man's Search for Meaning", shares his powerful experience and observations as a concentration camp survivor during the Nazi occupation. He became aware that, although the Nazis could control his environment, his food, his body and every external aspect of his life, they could not control his internal being. He, and he alone, had the ability to choose what he would think, how he would process his experiences, and what attitude he would adopt in response to the things that were being done to him. He noted that there was always a brief time gap between what he experienced and his response to that experience. In the gap was the power of choice. It enabled him to experience a tremendous freedom that in turn allowed him to survive the horror of that time.

He also noticed that the people who survived were the ones who nurtured thoughts that fostered hope. It was the prisoners who lost hope who usually did not survive. There are many stories from that tragic era that powerfully demonstrate that the ability to choose one's attitude is the crux of the deepest and most profound type of freedom.

Another example is that of Wild Bill Cody. He was given that moniker because he looked a bit like Wild Bill Hickock. He was a prisoner in a concentration camp in World War II. When people first saw him they often assumed he hadn't been there for very long because he was energetic and full of life. But in reality he had been in the Wuppertal camp for years, and lived on the same meager subsistence as the rest of the prisoners. But he seemed impervious to the mental, emotional and even physical deterioration from which the other prisoners suffered. He always seemed to have time, a smile and a compassionate word for whoever had need. He treated everyone with kindness and patience.

When liberation day came he encouraged fellow prisoners to refrain from killing the German people in revenge for former atrocities. He encouraged forgiveness and kindness. When he was faced with a lack of understanding, he shared his story. He had lived in Warsaw before his imprisonment. When the German soldiers rolled into his town they lined his wife, two daughters and three sons up against a wall and shot them. He begged to die with them, but was denied that relief. Seeing the fruits of such hate, he made the decision to spend the rest of his life loving every person with which he came into contact. Making the choice to love energized his life. It was not an easy choice, or a convenient one, but it made a difference to everyone he met. And it was the choice to love in the presence of hate that kept him vigorous and healthy.

Nelson Mandela also discovered internal freedom during his imprisonment for more than 27 years when apartheid reigned in South Africa. One of the things he shared about that experience was "I am fundamentally an optimist. Whether that comes from nature or nurture, I cannot say. Part of being optimistic is keeping one's head pointed toward the sun, one's feet moving forward. There were many dark moments when my faith in humanity was sorely tested, but I would not and could not give myself up to despair. That way lays defeat and death." And when he was released from prison he said about that moment, "As I walked out the door toward the gate that would lead to my freedom, I knew if I didn't leave my bitterness and hatred behind, I'd still be in prison." As a result he helped to heal a nation and inspire the world.

Choosing your attitude is not easy. It takes self-honesty, practice, patience and persistence. But the capacity to choose your attitude can be developed and learned.

Some people have developed emotional set points - emotional tendencies that tend to stay within a relatively narrow range. There may be some fluctuation due to life events but the emotional levels of intensity are fairly uniform over time. These are habituated emotional patterns. But they can be changed by developing and practicing new habits. Chemical and brain changes occur with each choice you make about where you place your focus and attention. Focusing on positive, joyful thoughts and feelings over time create new neuro-pathways in the brain and a new emotional set-point. Old neuro-pathways that carried negative thoughts and painful emotions begin to weaken when attention is removed from them. It's like allowing a well-worn pathway in a field to become overgrown from lack of use, while stomping down the grass and creating a new path that is easy to traverse.

All emotions have a purpose, even those that may create some discomfort.

Anger: Sometimes anger is categorized as a 'negative' emotion. However, there is a purpose and appropriate use for anger. Anger can help galvanize you to take action when necessary. It gives you the energy you need to respond if healthy boundaries are seriously transgressed. The problem occurs when anger is habituated. This can happen if you sublimate the anger instead of taking appropriate action and making healthy changes.

Anger can also become physically and emotionally addictive. The emotion of anger elicits powerful chemicals and hormones in the body. If anger is frequently indulged it can create an addiction, causing you to consciously or subconsciously create, or allow circumstances into your life that trigger an angry response. If anger is a frequent part of your life it may be helpful to assess whether you might be addicted to the emotion of anger.

Fear: People can find themselves in a downward spiral of fear. Fear has a lot of code names. Some are worry, anxiety, shyness, nervousness and stress. I consider all of these emotions along the continuum of fear.

Fear, too, has a purpose - it is nature's way of keeping you vigilant and safe in the face of danger. It's good to be energized by fear if you walk outside and find an enormous, vicious bear running toward you. The part of your brain that bypasses your reasoning centers motivates you into immediate, life-saving action. This is helpful and empowering fear.

Fear, however, is often a thought habit that has been learned and developed over time. If it occurs too often it can begin to change brain chemistry and become chronic. This is the essence of an addiction. The good news is that chronic fear can be transformed through the power of alchemy.

"What if?" is a powerful question. People often begin a downward spiral of fear and worry with this question. I find it fascinating that "What if?" most often elicits negative musings. "What if the new management lays me off?"; "What if people hate my book?"; "What if I fail at this endeavor?"

The opposite questions are just as valid. "What if the new management absolutely loves me?"; "What if people love my book and it is incredibly successful?"; "What if I succeed in this endeavor beyond my wildest dreams?" You are making it all up in your mind anyway. None of it is reality yet. As long as you are making it up, consider making up a good "what if?".

There are some very illuminating definitions of worry that I have heard over the years. Worry is negative planning. Worry is having more faith in evil than in good. Worry is a misguided use of imagination. Whatever definition and perspective you take, worry is unproductive at best and destructive at worst. It can drain you of courage, creativity and ingenuity. It can cause you to be impotent, unable to respond with all your resources and energy.

Sadness: Everyone experiences sadness during times of disappointment and loss. For example, when a loved one dies sadness and a feeling of loss is natural. Sadness and grief can help us clarify what we value in life. But when feelings of grief, loss and sadness are not fully resolved they get stuck in the body, and depression may result.

Sadness, including depression and grief, can be strangely beguiling. Sometimes people may even feel guilty for ceasing to feel sad after a loved one dies. There may be an underlying belief that it is somehow a betrayal to ever feel joy again.

When you are profoundly sad or depressed, it may feel impossible to muster the energy to even *want* to feel better. There can almost be satisfaction in remaining miserable. Trying to feel better may just seem to highlight how miserable you feel.

Focusing excessively on painful emotions can increase their power and perpetuate them in your life. It can also begin to negatively change your brain and body chemistry, causing you to become addicted to the emotional state, as established by Dr. Candice Pert, author of Molecules of Emotion: The Science Behind Mind-Body Medicine".

This doesn't mean that painful emotions should be ignored, suppressed or repressed. They just shouldn't be given the power to dictate your life and rob you of joy. The way to heal is not to deny your feelings, but rather to observe them objectively, understand their message and bring love and compassion to them. Just as physical pain imparts information that something needs attention; all emotional pain has a message. Observing your emotions allows you to hear their message so that you can take helpful steps to bring healing.

Why don't people automatically adopt paradigms that create the life they want? While you can choose and change your paradigms, it usually must be done intentionally; otherwise you default to those you were taught, grew up with and extracted from your life and experiences. Before you can intentionally change your paradigms you need to understand what your current paradigms are, and what has been impeding more helpful perspectives. Observing your thoughts on a regular basis, especially during meditation, can help you begin to discover your underlying thought patterns and paradigms.

Observing your thoughts objectively can be challenging. Intense emotional pain can be blinding. It can be easy to be swept away in whatever emotional current rushes by. There is a difference, however, between standing at the river's edge and watching the turmoil of the current, and being hurled about *in* the current. It's helpful to engage in daily practices that allow you to keep your footing when difficulties seem to inundate your life.

One way to ensure you don't find yourself sinking in the midst of instability is to engage in a daily meditative practice. Meditation is time when you get quiet enough to gain clarity about what is going on in your life, thoughts and emotions. When you meditate, you have the opportunity to connect with a greater wisdom within yourself than you might when you are distracted by the busyness of life.

Sometimes you may be unaware of unresolved issues in your life that are causing you to experience physical or emotional pain. This can stem from the desire to bury the past. Burying the past is important, but if you bury it alive it can reach up and grab you unexpectedly.

It is a commonly held belief that in order to truly bury the past you have to focus on each individual trauma. I have not found this to be either true or productive. While it can be helpful to understand the source of your internal responses to external triggers, it is also important to not focus overly much on the pain of the past. It can keep you stuck and cause the energy of past painful experiences to expand and consume.

What you focus on tends to grow in power. Instead, become clear about what you want to believe and replace the old beliefs systems in your mind with healthier and more empowering belief systems.

There is a parable that crosses cultures and appears in various forms. In Chinese culture it is two dogs, but the story line is essentially the same:

"A grandfather is teaching his grandson about life. A terrible fight is going on inside of me, inside of you and inside of every person. It is a terrible fight between two dogs. One is an angry, arrogant, resentful, depressed and fear-filled dog and the other is a joyful, loving, faithful and content dog. Which one wins?

"The answer is the one you feed! The other dog dies a natural death from starvation."

You are not your past. Your history is the sum of your experiences, encounters and choices. You are much more than a mere combination of these factors. You are also not your pain. You are, in each moment, pure potential. The science of quantum physics now tells us that everything in the universe, including us, is pure potential. When people have been in emotional and/or physical pain for a long enough period of time, they often begin to identify with it. I frequently hear people say things like, "I *am* a sinner." "I *am* stupid." "I *am* a disabled person." "I *am* angry." "*My* fibromyalgia." But none of these are truly who and what you are. They are things you are experiencing. They are not *you*.

Another way in which to reduce chronic feelings of stress is to lower your tolerance for stress. At first blush this may seem a bit counter-intuitive, but it can help reduce your experience of stress. Sometimes people allow stress into their life by their action and/or inaction. In other words, stress is often allowed too much of a foothold.

Have you ever observed, or experienced this scene in a grocery store?

> Child: "Can I have some candy?"
> Parent: "No, not today."
> Child (stomping feet and declaring loudly): "But I want candy!"
> Parent: "No, I said not today. Now don't ask me again!"
> Child (screaming at the top of his or her lungs): "I WANT CANDY!"
> Parent: "I SAID DON'T ASK ME AGAIN!!!"
>   And on it goes…

There will, of course, be times when a child can be difficult to communicate with because they are overly tired or distressed. In this example the situation might have turned out differently if the parent had been pro-active sooner – even leaving the store if necessary.

Another way to reduce tolerance for stress is to stop overcommitting. Overcommitting is an invitation for stressful feelings. Learning to say "no" is a powerful way to maintain balance in your life. Gandhi stated, "There is more to life than increasing its speed."

Reducing your tolerance for stress is honoring the need for a balanced life. It requires being pro-active rather than reactive in your approach. Setting healthy boundaries, instead of trying to power through an overcommitted schedule helps minimize feelings of stress. If you often feel too busy and overwhelmed, you may be tolerating and accepting too much stress into your life. Lowering your tolerance for stress is making a conscious choice to not accommodate avoidable stressors in your life.

A balanced life is the result of balanced choices. You can't take on too much responsibility, neglect self-care, tolerate abusive behavior from others, and still experience a life of balance. Placing a high premium on living with balance will prompt you to take appropriate action when something threatens to compromise it.

It is also essential to let go of the idea that you can change somebody else. People often frustrate themselves by trying to control the thoughts or actions of others. It's easy to feel that if only "they" would change then life would be so much the better. Attempting to exert this type of control over others will inevitably create stressful feelings. In reality, your thoughts, actions and emotions may influence others, but generally this is a natural result of your example and state of being. The most powerful thing you can do to positively influence those around you is to live from a place of authentic love and compassion.

It's also important to accept where you currently are in your life. If you want to drive from your current location to New York, you must acknowledge and start from where you are. Refusing to do so will affect your chance of getting there. There's no need to be ashamed of where you are in life. It's simply where you are. Buckminster Fuller said, "You can never change things by fighting the existing reality. To change something, build a new model that makes the existing model obsolete." You can't cause darkness to flee a room by flailing at it, but only by introducing light. But you must also recognize and acknowledge that you are standing in darkness before you can make a choice to bring in light. Emotional wounds are not healed by denial, judgment or self-condemnation. They are healed by love, compassion and acceptance.

Chapter 5

Tiered-believability Affirmations

"It's the repetition of affirmations that leads to belief. And once that belief becomes a deep conviction, things begin to happen." Muhammad Ali

"Belief precedes all action." James Allen

Your self-concept is who you believe yourself to be. It is a collection of ideas about yourself that you constructed based on what you heard and were told by significant people in your life. These ideas are generally based on other people's personal preferences, biases and expectations. Those perspectives may or may not reflect who you choose to be. How you view yourself is pivotal because you can only consistently behave in ways that are congruent with how you see yourself. If you see yourself as a jerk, then you won't be able to behave any other way for very long. If you see yourself as an idiot, you will frequently find yourself behaving like an idiot. If you perceive yourself as a kind and loving person, then your behavior will generally reflect that viewpoint. You will subconsciously self-sabotage if your self-concept is worse than your current circumstances, because you don't believe you deserve your success. If you aren't living congruently with your image of yourself, you must either change the image or change the behavior to maintain the image. Tiered-believability affirmations can help you shift into a new self-image paradigm.

You may have tried using affirmations in the past without much success. You may have found that you couldn't continue saying affirmations because you felt like every word was a big fat lie. It can feel impossible to try to convince yourself that you are "grateful to be a slender and healthy 128 pounds", if every time you look in the mirror all you see is an unhealthy 350 pound person. Repeating, "I am in perfect health.", if you can barely crawl out of bed every morning because you feel so poorly, can be frustrating. Saying, "I am wealthy and have financial abundance!", when you barely have enough money to buy food, can feel like it actually underscores your dire straits. This chapter presents a simple, practical way of approaching affirmations that will enhance success. It is easy to learn and sustain because you will believe every word you are saying. As a result, you will experience positive results faster than you thought possible.

Tiered-believability affirmations are a way in which you can learn to think in empowering ways about yourself, other people, your experiences and the world in general. It's a way of creating the emotions, attitudes and life you desire. Using affirmations is often minimized, or dismissed as ineffective; however, incredible results can be realized with a few modifications to the traditional approach.

Tiered-believability affirmations need to have all of the following components in order to optimize results. I have approached the affirmations like a recipe. A recipe requires specific, individual ingredients in correct measurement. If you were making a cake it would be understood that each ingredient in isolation can't produce the desired result of a tasty and delicious dessert. This is also true for affirmations. Each ingredient is necessary, but they all work together to create success.

Tiered-believability affirmations should be personal. Wording should refer to you specifically, rather than just a general statement. Words such as "I", "me", "mine" and the use of your name are essential. An example of a personally worded affirmation is "I, Diane, am happy!"

Tiered-believability affirmations should be positively worded. Affirmations should always be worded positively because what you focus on tends to increase in your life. If your affirmation is "I no longer smoke cigarettes", your subconscious mind hears the words "smoke cigarettes". The result is that you will want to smoke. A more useful affirmation would be "I, Diane, now am choosing to develop healthy, clean and strong lungs."

Tiered-believability affirmations should be present tense. Present tense words are words like "now" "currently", "presently", and "am". It can also include any present- tense verb such as "I feel", "I believe", etc. A present tense affirmation might be, "I *am now* healthy and I *feel* great!" Phrases like "I *will be* healthy" keeps the realization of the goal continually in the future. When I put this recipe together later I'll explain how you can utilize a "Tiered-Believability" technique so the statements you develop can be present-tense as well as believable to you.

Tiered-believability affirmations should be visual. Visualizing as part of your affirming is essential. Much research has been done on the effectiveness of using visualization to enhance performance and facilitate change. Studies reveal the same brain patterns occur while visualizing yourself performing an activity as when actually performing the activity. In one study an exercise psychologist from the Cleveland Clinic Foundation in Ohio found that participants who used only mental visualization of lifting weights increased their muscle strength by almost half that of those who actually lifted weights.[4] Visualization actually has a physiological effect on the body. Visualization mimics action. Affirmations that have been enhanced with visualizations are a way of living from the desired end rather than moving into the desired experience. Visualized affirmations help you to see, feel and experience the outcome even before it happens. As a result, neurological, bio-chemical and energetic changes occur that help draw what you want into your direct experience.

Tiered-believability affirmations should be emotionally charged. The more emotion that accompanies an affirmation, the more powerful it will be. An emotionally charged affirmation will enable you to shift to a more empowered mindset much more quickly than with an affirmation that is emotionally tepid. It has been said that we make decisions based on emotion and then we justify them with rationalization.

Emotions are the fuel of our lives. Emotion is what motivates us and moves us to action, or causes us to remain stuck in fear. Just watch a sports movie like *Remember the Titans* to witness the power emotion can evoke. In one scene they huddle together and loudly chant "Left side – Strong side!" Can you imagine if they had all huddled together and muttered this sentence with a lethargic monotone? They passionately, and with all their being, shouted, *"LEFT SIDE – STRONG SIDE!"* Emotions turbo-charge an affirmation.

Tiered-believability affirmations should have supporting evidence. Supporting evidence makes an affirmation more believable. It validates the statement. "Because" is the pivotal word when building an affirmation that has supporting evidence. Saying "I am healthy and strong" may feel less believable than "I am healthy and strong *because* I am choosing to nourish my body with healthy food and exercise daily".

Tiered-believability affirmations should be used regularly and often. Your current thoughts and feelings have their roots in your past experiences. Change in these areas doesn't happen by accident. It is important to be deliberate and persistent. Remember, your current way of thinking and default perspectives are mental habits. They can change, they just need time.

Thoughts and feelings move along established neuro-pathways in the brain. The more often you entertain a thought, the more entrenched and significant the neuro-pathway becomes.

Tiered-believability affirmations should include motion. Emotions and motion are closely aligned. Anthony Robbins, a well-known life strategist, says motion generates emotion. Research into the connection between physiology and emotion supports this assertion.[5] For example, smiling in a way that engages the muscles around the eyes will instantly cause hormonal and chemical changes in the body that improve mood. Making a fist when you feel fearful will increase feelings of courage and determination. A frown will instantly increase feelings of sadness, as will holding your shoulders in a stooped, depressed-looking position. Saying your affirmations while assuming body positions and facial expressions that support the affirmations will make an enormous difference. Additionally, saying your affirmations aloud can help the desired messages register in your subconscious mind.

Tiered-believability affirmations should be used at the optimal time. There are optimal times to say affirmations. Two of the most important times are first thing in the morning and right before bed. Saying affirmations when you first wake-up and as you drift off to sleep allows your subconscious mind to more easily accept them. These are the times when your conscious mind is less apt to try to judge and shout down a paradigm-changing affirmation. Replacing negative self-talk with a positive affirmation is important. It is also helpful to repeat your affirmations as often as possible, especially in the beginning. The goal is to saturate your entire being with the affirmation so that it becomes part of who you are. Don't be discouraged if you don't have profound results immediately, affirmations are the seeds of change.

Tiered-believability affirmations should be charged with rhythm: Rhythm helps affirmations bypass some of the filtering and guarding of the conscious mind. For example, if I sing "I feel good…da da da da da da da…like I knew that I would…da da da da da da da…" my conscious mind is unlikely to filter it as strictly - because it is a *song* - but my subconscious mind is hearing me say over and over that I feel good. This can be profound since it can make the subconscious more receptive. For a long time I set the words "I love myself" to music. I sang it in my mind almost all the time. I had my own tune, but when I went into a store, I would sing the words to whatever music they were playing as well. Setting my affirmations to music caused the affirmations to get stuck in my head. Even now I sometimes spontaneously sing that old phrase, even though I moved on to other affirmations long ago. The affirmation has become part of me. Even if you don't choose to put your affirmation to music, creating a cadence or rhythm can also create a somewhat hypnotic effect, allowing the subconscious mind to more easily accept the new affirmation.

Tiered-believability affirmations should be believable to you. I know this one goes against the commonly held belief that an affirmation should only reflect the end result, such as "I *am now* perfectly healthy and filled with vitality!" However, if you are currently experiencing a substantial health challenge, there will likely be a tremendous amount of mental resistance to the idea that you are *now* healthy and vital. Sometimes the gap between where you currently are and where you want to be is just too great. If you are unemployed and barely scraping by financially, saying "I am now financially well-off and abundantly wealthy" can actually trigger a loud voice in the back of your head that screams back, "*Are you kidding me?! What a crock!*" Affirmations of this nature might eventually work if repeated often enough and for long enough a period of time –but it can be a bit like trying to swim upstream. The force and direction of the water creates resistance that impedes your progress upstream. There is a faster and more efficient way that circumvents the internal conflict of repeating statements you don't really believe. Remember, it's not what you say, but what you believe and feel that makes the difference. Tiered-believability' can produce results more quickly and more easily.

Tiered-believability affirmations help you cross the chasm from where you currently are to where you want to be. Word your affirmations to reflect what you want to create, yet in a way that feels authentic and stretches your current belief structure. Some examples are:

- **Tiered-believability example A:** Mary has been told by her family her whole life that she is worthless and will amount to nothing. She finds that message permeates every aspect of her life. She has never succeeded in any endeavor that was truly important to her. She knows that if she believed in herself more, her life would be much richer and she would be more likely to experience success. She decides to try some affirmations to change her sense of self-worth.

She tries:

1. "I am completely worthy of good things in my life and can experience success in the things that are important to me." *She doesn't believe it for a moment. The little voice in her head shouts her down quickly and mercilessly.*

2. "I choose to believe I am worthy of good things in my life and can experience success in the things that are important to me if I work hard enough." *This is not quite as hard a step to accept, but the little voice is still pretty loud.*

3. "I believe it is **possible** that I am worthy of good things in my life and can experience success in the things that are important to me." *This is believable but a stretch. She still experiences some discomfort with the idea of being worthy and successful, but hey, **anything** is possible – right? This affirmation will allow her to take a step in the direction she wants. Once she feels comfortable and has fully assimilated this affirmation then she may move on to #2.*

- **Tiered-believability example B:** John, age 26, has struggled with obesity since he was a teen. His ideal weight is 185 pounds, but he currently weighs 326 pounds. He is feeling discouraged and hopeless. He has tried every diet imaginable. Nothing has worked for him. He has heard that maybe he could have a chance if he changed his thoughts

He tries:

1. "I am happy and excited to weigh 185 pounds." *He feels like he is telling himself an outright lie. His finds it impossible to not internally scoff at the idea that he **now** weighs in at his ideal weight.*

2. "I choose to believe that I am now at my ideal weight of 185 pounds." *No better.*

3. "I choose to believe that I am now capable of getting to my ideal weight of 185 pounds. Others have done it, and what is possible for one person is possible for me." *Ahh. This one works. It helps him take the step out of hopelessness and victimhood into personal empowerment. Again, once he has said this affirmation often enough that he fully believes it, he may move on to the second affirmation in this example above.*

- **Tiered-believability example C:** Jennifer is flat broke. She works a minimum wage job and barely ekes out enough to pay her living expenses. She remembers as a child often hearing phrases like, "Money doesn't grow on trees" and "Money is the root of all evil." A friend suggested to her that her financial situation may be connected with those beliefs. She decides she no longer wants to accept the messages about finances she was taught as a child. She wants her subconscious beliefs to reflect an easier relationship with money.

She tries:

1. "I am abundantly wealthy and financially free." *This statement immediately gives rise to loud internal objection.*

2. "I believe I deserve financial wealth and abundance" *She finds herself not believing this at all. As a matter of fact since money is the root of all evil, to deserve it would mean she too is evil.*

3. "The more I have, the more I can give. I open myself to abundance so that I can give generously. " *This statement meets no resistance. Once she fully accepts this affirmation she may choose to move on to the second option in this example.*

- **Tiered-believability example D:** Justin has lived with intense anxiety his whole life. There have only been a few fleeting times in his life when he didn't feel anxious and on-edge. He wants to begin to feel more peace and joy in his life. A friend suggested he begin daily affirmations. Justin feels just desperate enough to try.

He tries:

1. "I feel a sense of joy and peace in my life." *Not!*

2. "I believe it is possible to experience joy and peace in my life." *He doesn't believe it is possible to experience joy and peace. He doesn't even know why he is bothering with this at all. Rather than experiencing hope with these words, he finds they elicit feelings of despair.*

3. "Peace. Joy. " *He doesn't attach himself at all to the words. For now he is unable to even personalize the statements. That will come next. For now just the words "peace" and "joy" will begin to create a resonance inside of him. For him it is the first step. The next step might be to ask himself the question, "What would it be like if I felt at peace and joyful?"*

Now, let's put the affirmation ingredients together to make a few powerful Tiered-believability example recipes. Ideally only two or three should be utilized at a time. Repeating too many on a daily basis can become time consuming and water down the desired results. Choosing a few pivotal affirmations to use over a period of time focuses intention in a more powerful, laser-like way. A few examples of fully developed affirmations are:

- "I, Diane, love that I can remember names easily because I am deciding to give my full attention to a person's name when they are introduced."

- "I, Frank, am so excited that money comes so easily to me because I choose to give, and I trust that it will flow back to me."

- "I, Jennifer, live joyfully because I choose to take time to appreciate the wonderful people and experiences in my life."

- "My health is vibrant because I take time to exercise, eat well and enjoy life."

- "I, Tom, feel great because I am choosing to appreciate the good things in my life!"

- "I, Tameka, feel incredibly relaxed and at peace because I am choosing to take the time to meditate daily.

- "I, Borg, am so grateful that I am richly abundant on every level because God and the Universe conspire to bless me."

- "I, Angela, feel amazing and have incredible energy because I nourish and care for my body and spirit."

- "I, Alessandro, love my life because I choose to focus on all of my blessings and gifts."

- "I, Zhou, am excited to create the life that I want because I am an awesomely creative being."

- "My intuition and spiritual insight are tremendous because I continually develop and refine them."

- "I, Liam, look forward to every day with joy and excitement because each day is an opportunity to learn and grow."

- "I, Levi, am profoundly happy because I choose to be so."

- "I, Anna, am eternally safe because I am more than my body - and nothing can harm my spirit."

- "I, Maiko, choose to love myself because I am a unique expression of the Divine."

- "I, Arthur, love my job because it gives me the opportunity to share my gifts with others."

Tiered-believability affirmations work. I know because they changed my life. I believe they can change yours, too. If you develop and repeat your affirmations at least two to three times a day (more will produce faster results), you will begin to experience changes. In the beginning the changes may be subtle; however, after a few weeks you will begin to notice a shift in your thoughts and feelings. For severe issues that have persisted over many years it may take a while longer, but persistence will make a difference. It is a sure thing that whatever you focus on grows. I wish you a bountiful harvest!

Chapter 6

Somatics

"The body tells a story. It is, in fact, a living autobiography". Elaine Mayland

"Pain is the body's cry for help. You are doing something that the body can't take any longer. The body is very patient. It takes a lot of tension and abuse before it makes pain." Marion Rosen

The word "somatic" is from the Greek root soma, which means "the living organism in its wholeness." A simple definition is "of the body". When faced with difficult situations people often dissociate with their body as a coping strategy. Let's face it, painful emotions are not an enjoyable experience. It's human nature to try to avoid pain and optimize pleasure. Sadness, anger, frustration, regret, fear and other uncomfortable emotions have traditionally been viewed as inherently negative, and indicative of a character defect. Nothing could be further from the truth. Every emotion has a purpose. It is important to avoid blocking out even painful emotions. If you block painful emotions, then you automatically block the joyful ones as well.

No emotion is inherently bad. Emotions can help you make choices that will move you in the direction you desire. Anger provides you the energy and fire necessary to take action when your boundaries are crossed. Fear provides you the motivation to make choices and decisions that help ensure your safety and survival. And sadness helps you clarify and put into perspective things in your life that you truly value.

The difficulty arises when you deny or subjugate your feelings. Physical symptoms will inevitably occur. Emotions that are hidden or repressed have immense power to control you without your consent. In Chinese Medicine there is no such thing as a bad emotion. Emotions only cause harm if they become fixed in the body, or are expressed in an uncontrolled or hurtful way. Emotional balance results from accepting and feeling your emotions, and then allowing them to flow through you to be discharged and released in a mindful and responsible manner. Recognizing and acknowledging the truth of how you feel is the first step in understanding what you need in order to heal. If you block or disconnect from your feelings, you limit your ability to process them, learn from them and move on.

I used to be confused about how this concept fit in with the Law of Attraction. The Law of Attraction asserts that whatever emotions or thoughts you entertain will draw more of the same into your life. In other words, the more angry emotions or thoughts you allow, the more situations you will attract into your life that feed your anger. The more you allow for depressed thoughts, the more sadness you will draw to you, etc. I believed simply thinking about or feeling painful emotions would draw more of that emotional experience. What I now understand is that it goes deeper than that.

There is a caveat to the Law of Attraction that is often unrecognized or acknowledge. *What you attract into your life will be what you truly and honestly feel and believe from the deepest part of yourself, not what you superficially assert as true. You cannot attract the things and experiences you want into your life from an inauthentic, dissociated state of being.* If you are mentally affirming peace, but you are sublimating the emotion of fear, you will *not* be attracting peace into your life because you are actually living in an unrecognized and unresolved state of fear. Because you are living in fear, you will be attracting fearful experiences into your life.

This is monumentally important. The nature of emotions is that they must be felt - thus the term "feelings". If they are not felt on an emotional level, they will be stored and felt physically in your body. Patients frequently tell me they store their emotions in their shoulders (or back, or jaws, etc.). And, of course, the result is that they are experiencing pain and discomfort in that region of their body. The emotion is not gone, it is simply stuck in the body and expressing itself in a different way – and will continue to do so until it is processed and released.

Your body can be seen as your biography. There is much to be learned by reconnecting to the wisdom that your body has to share. You may have learned to dissociate from your body in order to avoid confronting and dealing with the painful emotions in your life. I find it interesting that even word choices often reflect the body-emotion connection. People who use the phrase, "that is such a headache!" often experience headaches. People who feel overwhelmed and express that "it is too much to bear!" often have shoulder pain and tension. People who say, "What a pain in the neck!" often store their emotions in the neck, etc.

It is important to feel and process your emotions in an authentic and responsible way so that they don't get stuck in your body. Your exterior and interior experiences must be congruent. If they are not aligned, it will be your interior beliefs, unresolved emotions and stored pain that run the show. That's what dictates the direction and quality of your life and experiences.

How can you deal with your painful emotions, process them responsibly, release them and prevent them from getting stuck? How do you ensure that your internal and external belief systems are congruent? How do you make sure that what you are attracting to you will reflect what you desire, instead of being the result of some sublimated, unknown internal state of being? The answer to those questions is the key to a much more joyful, authentic and abundant life. Some steps that will help you do that include:

Don't Resist. I know this sounds counterintuitive; but it is an essential part of not getting stuck in pain. There is a saying that, "whatever you resist, persists." When you think about it more deeply it begins to make sense. When you resist something it becomes the object of your focus, and whatever you place your focus on tends to be what you move toward. A former parachute jumper once told me this story about his training experience in school: In preparation for their first jump experience the trainees were shown the field in which they would land. It was a very large field that was completely empty, save one lone, skinny tree. They were instructed to avoid the tree at all costs. Inevitably, the vast majority of them headed straight for the tree anyway. Why? The tree was the focus of their attention.

When you resist your experience, you perpetuate it and cause more of it to come into your life. How is this possible? Newtonian Law of Physics states "To every action there is an equal and opposite reaction". The ramification here is that when you resist something there will be an equal and opposite force from whatever you are resisting. What happens when you have two equal and opposite forces pushing against each other? Entropy. Stuckness. Lack of movement and flow. Resisting your emotions results in emotional entropy, the emotion stops flowing and gets stuck in your body.

Observe the emotion and accompanying thoughts without judgment. See and observe what you are experiencing without labeling it "good" or "bad". Just notice what is. You might note, "Oh, I see anger." You might notice feelings of frustration, or sadness. Observe the emotions as if they were objects. This will provide some space between you and the emotion so that you can clearly see your experience without being consumed by it.

49

For thousands of years Eastern spiritual traditions have taught this method as a strategy for mastering one's emotional life. In recent times studies have revealed this type of meditative practice positively impacts the neuro-pathways on which thoughts and emotions travel.[6] This means that over time, with regular practice, you will begin to minimize your habituated painful emotions and associated thought patterns because the pathways on which they travel weaken.

Observe your physical responses. You have the opportunity to learn how your body is reacting to your emotional experience. Scan your body with an awareness of your emotion. Does your jaw feel clenched or at ease? Is your chest at ease or tight? Does your stomach feel relaxed or tense? Are your buttocks squeezed tightly or comfortable? Scan and notice every part of your body. Your head, eyes, brows, jaws, shoulders, chest, stomach, back, abdominal area, buttocks, arms, hands, legs, feet, etc. Find and note any tension, discomfort, pain or restriction. If you find anything just notice and observe it for a few minutes. Don't rush off to the next part of your body to get away from it. Stay with it a little while. Don't resist it or run away. It has information for you. A gift. Open yourself to it. Accept it. Don't try to change it. Just feel it for a little while. Maybe even have a conversation with it. Ask it if it has anything it wants to say to you. Listen respectfully. It may tell you something that will be transformative. My stomach once said to me, "Why are you angry at me all the time for hurting? *I'm* not doing it to *you…you* are doing it to *me!*

You are not loving and taking care of me". When I thought about it, it was true. I had been angry with my stomach for hurting all the time, but failed to realize that I was injuring it with my terrible food choices.

Breathe. Breathing is an important cue and regulator of the stress response. If, for example, you came face to face with a bear while hiking, your breath would immediately move up to your chest. This ensures you will have ready and sufficient oxygen with which to flee or fight. But chest breathing can also *trigger* a stress response and simulate the flight or fight physical response. Because chest breathing is a stress response, your body assumes there must be danger somewhere nearby. As a result, a cascade of various stress chemicals and hormones flood your bloodstream, eliciting stressful feelings. You can begin to release and calm stressful emotions by breathing into your diaphragm and abdominal area instead of your chest. This sends a message to your brain and nervous system that all is well and it can relax.

Offer the painful areas compassion. Don't resist emotions and the corresponding physical response. Be willing to sit with the emotion for a time so you can fully process it. Honor your feelings, and be willing to authentically acknowledge what you are experiencing. You cannot transform and grow emotionally and spiritually unless you begin exactly where you are. After noticing what you are feeling emotionally and physically, offer your love and support to any part of your body that is tight, uncomfortable or in distress. Offer it a prayer of healing. Offer that part of yourself compassion and grace. Ask for, and receive, forgiveness.

Allow your body to process and release stuck emotion. The next step is to allow your body time to process and discharge any stuck emotions. An effective strategy is to focus on the emotion and associated physical sensation and allow the energy to flow to and out of your hands and feet. As you do this you may notice a number of physical sensations. You may shake; you might get really hot or cold; you might have some spontaneous muscle movements as previously stuck areas begin to flow. Allow all of these physical manifestations to progress unimpeded. This is exactly what needs to happen. Though it can feel uncomfortable during the process, the benefits are tremendous. It will ensure that painful emotions don't lodge and get stored in your body. This process provides a method to help process and free those that are currently stuck.

Notice and be grateful for changes. After you have processed and released the painful emotion and physically stuck energy, note any difference in how you feel and take a moment to be grateful. This will help solidify the changes in your new emotional and physical state. Let your focus be on what feels subjectively better to you, not on what is still left. Let it be okay that this may take a while. Don't frustrate or disappoint yourself by expecting 30 years of stuck emotions to be released in one or two sessions. Be patient and compassionate with yourself.

A significant benefit of doing this type of work is living a life that is more authentic and congruent. Forced "positivity" that denies and suppresses how you really feel keeps you stuck. You can't fool your subconscious. It is only with honest and authentic relationships with yourself, others and the world around you that there is the possibility for true transformation. Only then is there enduring change.

Chapter 7

Meditation

"Feelings come and go like clouds in a windy sky. Conscious breathing is my anchor."
Thích Nhất Hạnh

"To understand the immeasurable, the mind must be extraordinarily quiet, still."
Jiddu Krishnamurti

Imagine you and a colleague are on your way to an important business meeting. It is imperative that you both arrive on time since the new CEO of the company will be there. As the car is speeding along you happen to notice the gas gauge is on empty. You mention this important fact to your colleague, but to your great surprise her response is, "Well, I'm not stopping for gas! I'm too busy driving!" You point out that you don't think there is enough gas to make it, but she still is unwilling to stop for gas because it will take too much time. This approach is clearly counter-productive, yet it's the way many people live their lives.

In our culture great emphasis is placed on achieving and doing, often to the exclusion of *being*. Slowing down, or stopping, allows you time to refuel, recover, regain perspective, and simply enjoy the ride. Tim Kreider, cartoonist and author, explains it beautifully, "Idleness is not just a vacation, an indulgence, or a vice. The space and quiet it provides is a necessary condition for standing back from life and seeing it whole. It is, paradoxically, necessary to getting work done."

In Chinese Medicine everything is a combination of yin and yang. Yin correlates to a more restful, quiet, restorative type of energy, while yang energy is more active, dynamic, and moving. Each must be in balance relative to the other. Excessive rest and entropy (yin energy) can quench the yang energy fire, leading to lethargy, fatigue and boredom. On the other hand, if there is an overabundance of activity and movement (yang energy) it can burn up the yin energy, causing burnout, fatigue and increased susceptibility to illness and injury. It is helpful to assess whether you need more yang or more yin activity in your daily schedule. If you feel you have little or no time to relax, then you probably need to add some yin activities to your life. If you are a couch potato, then some yang activities might serve you. And paradoxically, sometimes one is needed in order to support the other. For example, you may need more exercise (yang activity) in order to sleep better (yin activity). Or you may need more yin activity (sleep and meditation) in order to have the resources to support the yang activities (work and exercise) in your daily life. It can also be helpful to consider the balance within the yin and yang aspects, respectively. For example, if you meditate daily for one hour, but only sleep two hours every day, there may not be a balance *within* the yin aspect of life's activities. If you spend 8 hours working, but get no physical exercise, there may be no balance within the yang aspect. So there must be balance *within* each aspect as well as *between* the two aspects.

You can't live an imbalanced life and expect balanced results. If you don't stop for gas you will run out. All systems, including the human body, need to be in balance for optimal functionality. This necessitates a well-rounded approach to rest and work, stillness and motion, and meditation and activity.

Much research has been done on the benefits of meditation.[6] Some well-known benefits of meditation include:

- Enhanced levels of concentration
- Reduced feelings of stress
- Improved quality of sleep
- Normalization of blood pressure
- Improvement in personal relationships
- Overall improved health

It's so important to make time for daily meditation. It helps ensure that you have the necessary fuel (energy), balance and perspective with which to approach all your activities. Scheduling a consistent time for meditation can help make it a regular part of your lifestyle.

Just as stopping for gas actually enables you to get where you're going, meditating allows you time to gather steam that will propel you forward with greater ease. It will diminish feelings of stress, and improve your overall health.

If you have never meditated before, or have done so infrequently, you may wonder how to incorporate meditation into your daily life. There are a variety of ways meditation can be practiced. It can fit within the framework of any belief system, religious persuasion or ideology.

Meditative techniques tend to fall within one of two categories: concentrative, and non-concentrative. Concentrative techniques involve bringing your attention to something external during meditation, like a flame, music, a sound, or an image. Non-concentrative meditation means bringing your awareness to something internal, such as your breathing, or a specific part of your body. Meditation can utilize some combination of concentrative and non-concentrative techniques simultaneously. Experiment and find the approach that works best for you. If you have never practiced meditation before, here are some basic approaches that might be helpful in the beginning:

A Basic Seated Meditation: Sit in a comfortable position, either with your legs in a lotus position, or with your feet flat on the ground. Notice any thoughts that arrive in your mind without judging them. Each time you notice a thought, release it. Allow your mind to become quiet. Don't force it. Release all thoughts. This takes practice. As thoughts arise, simply notice them without judgment and let them go. This is commonly known as becoming an observer, or watcher, of your thoughts. Simply observing your thoughts without judgment begins to loosen the grasp the thought has on your life and emotions.

Focused Meditation: The classic focused meditation involves centering your attention on the breath. Other types of focused meditation include concentrating on an object or a sound, a word, or a feeling. The goal is to gently place your attention on whatever your focus is, without thinking thoughts about it. If thoughts arise, notice and release them, then return your attention to the object of your focus.

Spiritual Meditation: Spiritual meditation may be experienced as a listening form of prayer. There is a voice *within* you that doesn't come *from* your physical, temporal self. Each person may give that voice a different name – God, the Divine, Instinct. Whatever name you choose, in order to hear that voice, the internal the constant stream of thoughts, worries, and internal noise must be quieted. There may be a question of importance to which you seek an answer. This type of meditation involves opening your heart and spirit, and listening to the still, small voice within.

Moving Meditation: Moving meditation is a spiritual approach to exercise. Incredible changes occur in your body, brain and nervous system when meditating and exercising. Movement is a vital part of physical, emotional, mental, and even spiritual, health. This type of meditation involves engaging in a repetitive activity that helps to quiet the mind, such as gardening, artwork, Tai Chi, yoga, walking meditation, etc. A vital aspect of a moving meditation is complete attention and focus on the activity *in the moment*. Planning dinner, worrying about work or finances doesn't count. Your mind should be exclusively and totally focused feeling and experiencing the activity, not thinking thoughts – even thoughts about the activity.

Your body needs to move in order to stay healthy and balanced. Consider what happens to water when its flow is impeded. It becomes putrid, smelly and stagnant. Just as water needs to flow in order for it to remain healthy and unpolluted, so too does your energy need to flow.

Exercise and regular movement has been shown to improve mood, decrease feelings of stress, increase energy, balance hormones and bio-chemicals, and improve overall mental, physical and emotional health. It creates changes in your mind and body that help clear mental clutter, and help you reconnect to your body and essence.

Three of my favorite moving meditations include:

Yoga: Yoga is well-known for reducing stress, as well as stretching and relaxing the body. It is a helpful modality if approached with mindfulness and wisdom. Yoga should be approached with a spirit of personal compassion and connection to your body. Listening to your body's needs and limitations is vital in order to avoid injuring yourself. I have seen people get overly ambitious and hurt themselves with stretches and stances for which they are ill prepared. If you choose to do yoga, I encourage you to find an experienced, caring yoga teacher for instruction. Books and videos are not adequate, because small discrepancies in posture and weight distribution in your specific structure can make an enormous difference.

Qi Gong: Qi Gong, also spelled Chi Kung, is an ancient practice that integrates physical postures and movements, special breathing techniques, visualization, mental focus and intention. It is a method designed to help balance and strengthen the Qi, or energy of the body, thereby assisting in the natural healing process. It is extremely powerful and effective. Qi Gong is composed of two words: *Qi* (pronounced *Chee)*, which is usually translated as the life force, or vital energy, that flows through and makes up all things in the universe; and *Gong*, which refers to cultivated or practiced skill. Together they mean cultivating energy.

Qi Gong can be used to increase the Qi, or vital energy of the body, as well as to help heal it. You can also learn to store Qi for use when you have a special need, and also to help support others in their healing. Technically Tai Chi and Kung Fu are forms of Qi Gong. Qi Gong classes are available in most communities.

Tai Chi: Often called Tai Chi Chuan, Tai Chi originated as an ancient form of self- defense in China at least 2000 years ago. It's often described as a form of meditation in motion. Tai Chi helps connect the mind and body through gentle movements that are coordinated with the breath. This form of movement therapy teaches ways to move the body through space softly, in proper alignment and with all parts of the body working together in harmony. Tai Chi, when practiced regularly, significantly reduces stress, while increasing flexibility, energy, strength and coordination. It is a powerful way to connect the mind and body.

Regardless of which specific technique you employ, there are some principles that are found in almost all meditative practices. These include:

Nurture a quiet mind: Meditation helps foster a quiet, calm mind. It soothes the entire nervous system and significantly reducing feelings of stress over time. If you don't experience a lot of silence in your life, at first it may be difficult to turn off your mind. The thoughts that arise may be worrisome, fearful and insecure ones. That's typical because those are the kinds of thoughts that people often suppress or deny. Simply notice that you are thinking, and then bring your attention back to your breath, or whatever word, sound or image you have chosen. Over time you will be able to quiet your mind more easily and quickly.

Experience the Present Moment: Most of us have a tendency to spend a significant amount of mental and emotional energy worrying about the future and/or replaying the past. Most meditative practices help bring your attention to the present moment. Meditation can help you learn to experience each moment as it happens, then let it go and experience the next moment. This is important since stressful feelings come from future or past concerns. Mastering the ability to stay in the present moment allows you to live a relaxed and stress-free life.

Altered State of Consciousness: You naturally experience different states of consciousness throughout the day. Sleep and dreaming are two examples of naturally-occurring altered states of consciousness. Daydreaming, watching television, studying, reading, and a number of other regular daily activities all affect your state of consciousness. There is nothing abnormal or inherently 'occult' about it. Meditation is simply an intentional altered state of consciousness that can result in significant and positive changes. Regular meditation increases activity in the regions of the brain associated with happiness and a positive frame of mind.

Regular meditation can be life-changing, as well as a powerful way to help prevent and manage physical and emotional stress. It can bring balance to an otherwise hectic and busy life. If you feel you are too busy to meditate then it is even more important to take the time to do it. Even 5 to 10 minutes a day can make a substantial difference. Scheduling meditation at the same time every day can help you incorporate it into your lifestyle. Why not try it for one month and see the difference?

Chapter 8

Embracing Change

"Everyone thinks of changing the world, but no one thinks of changing himself." Leo Tolstoy

"Circumstances don't make the man, they only reveal him to himself". Epictetus

Change is inevitable. Each moment brings newness and transformation. Trying to resist change is a sure recipe for frustration. Feelings of stress arise when you resist change rather than accept and embrace it. But most of us tend to struggle against change, preferring to remain comfortably ensconced in the familiar. Change can bring a sense of insecurity in the face of the unknown. Sometimes we fear that change might herald unpleasant circumstances, or a negative shift in life. We prefer the known, even if it is less than ideal, to the unknown. It's challenging to trust in the natural unfolding of life, as well as in your own personal resources and resiliency.

One thing that creates a barrier to embracing change is judging situations as positive or negative from a short-term perspective. We often label a situation as positive or negative based on our own estimate of the situation. If we like it, it is deemed positive. If we dislike it, it is determined to be negative. We judge based on our own level of comfort. If we're comfortable, it's considered positive. If we're uncomfortable, it's regarded as negative. But haven't we all had the experience of thinking a situation was catastrophic, only to later realize it was actually a blessing? Consider this famous Taoist story of an old farmer:

The farmer had worked his crops for many years. One day his horse ran away. Upon hearing the news, his neighbors came to visit. "Such bad luck," they said sympathetically. "May be," the farmer replied. The next morning the horse returned, bringing with it three other wild horses. "How wonderful," the neighbors exclaimed. "May be," replied the old man. The following day, his son tried to ride one of the untamed horses, was thrown, and broke his leg. The neighbors again came to offer their sympathy on his misfortune. "May be," answered the farmer. The day after, military officials came to the village to draft young men into the army. Seeing that the son's leg was broken, they passed him by. The neighbors congratulated the farmer on how well things had turned out. "May be," said the farmer.

In this parable the farmer was always looking at the big picture rather than isolated incidents. Looking at the big picture allows you to have a wiser and more balanced perspective. It fosters hope when you are able to trust that things generally work together for the best over time.

I recently read a true story of how a major, and seemingly horrific, change in a man's life turned out to be the greatest opportunity imaginable. Shin Dong-Hyuk is the only person ever born in a North Korean prison camp known to escape. His incredible story is told in the book "Escape from Camp 14". His life in Camp 14 was a living nightmare; filled with physical, mental and emotional torture of unimaginable proportions. At one point he was lucky enough to be assigned to work on the farm. This was considered the most desired job in the camp because it afforded the opportunity to steal food. Starvation was commonplace in the camp, and food was a scarce and well-guarded commodity. As a farm worker he had the pleasure of being able to work outside in the fresh air and sunlight. He could also steal small bits of food unnoticed. If he was lucky, he could sneak some of the kernels of corn that were passed undigested into the cows' feces. He considered himself lucky. When he was unexpectedly transferred to the garment factory he felt like his world fell apart. The garment factory was a ticket to the graveyard. It was a dark, dank place with fetid, putrid smelling air. Death from starvation was commonplace. He was devastated!

After working in the factory for a short while, he met another prisoner who had lived and worked for many years in South Korea. This prisoner began to tell Shin Dong-Hyuk about the world outside the prison camp, a world that Shin Dong-Hyuk had never even known existed. He had assumed that the prison camp was the entire world, since it was all he had ever experienced. He began hearing about things like freedom and independence. Shin Dong-Hyuk learned about a world where there was plenty of food and where torture wasn't the norm. He listened; he learned… he began to dream.

Shin Dong-Hyuk began to plan his escape, and eventually was successful. The transfer to the garment factory – the very event he initially considered the most devastating thing that could have happened – turned out to be the first step on his path to freedom.

Most situations aren't as dramatic as the above example - but accepting change, and the gifts and potential opportunities afforded by change, can help you make powerful shifts in your life. Resistance keeps you stuck and frustrated. Every situation has within it a seed of opportunity. Sometimes that opportunity is simply to grow, learn and evolve. It's not always fun, but if you are open to change, it is always worthwhile.

As I learned from one of my Chinese teachers in grad school, the Chinese symbol for crisis is also the symbol for opportunity. I know that seems like a cliché, but sometimes clichés are true. If your response to a situation is one of trust, with intent to find and make the best from the situation, then the unfolding will be constructive. If your response is one of fear, with a hyper-focus on your pain, then the unfolding will likely perpetuate the pain you are experiencing.

The opportunity is in the response. You may feel you had no choice in getting to where you currently are in life, but you do have a choice in how you respond to whatever it is you are facing. There is an opportunity to learn and grow from every experience and encounter, whether it was planned or not.

Change is the nature of all life. Resistance never moves you in the direction that you want; it keeps you stuck in pain. It's like the child's toy commonly called "Chinese finger torture". You put your finger into the small woven tube, but the harder you then try to pull it out the more stuck your finger becomes. The only way to extract your finger is to simply relax. Then the tube is easily removed. Another real life example is insomnia. Desperately trying to fall asleep is actively resisting the current state of wakefulness. The irony is that the more you resist your state of wakefulness, the more elusive sleep becomes. It's like chasing a butterfly.

Being open to change allows your life to flow, keeping your energy fresh and healthy. Consider what happens to a stream if the flow becomes blocked. Standing puddles of water become stagnant and rank. A fresh stream of moving water is necessary to sustain the life and health of the stream. So too is flow, or change, needed in your life. Embracing, and trusting the process of change, which is the essence of life, is an essential aspect of personal alchemy.

Chapter 9

Gratitude

"It is not how much we have, but how much we enjoy that makes happiness."
Charles Spurgeon

"Piglet noticed that even though he had a Very Small Heart, it could hold a rather large amount of Gratitude." A.A. Milne, Winnie-the-Pooh

Gratitude is an essential part of living from an empowered and joyful paradigm. Ingratitude, on the other hand, creates a sense of dissatisfaction and lack. Being thankful is primarily a matter of perspective. Consider, for example, Ralph. Ralph hated his job. He worked in a restaurant as a waiter, complaining incessantly about the hours, the pay, the bad tips and the cantankerous customers. But when the restaurant went bankrupt he lost his job. He searched for weeks to find another position. He found himself wishing for the days when he had a steady, dependable paycheck. What had previously felt burdensome now became attractive. He felt intense gratitude when, a couple of months later, he found a job at another restaurant - even though the pay, hours and customers were all very similar to the job he had before.

A few years ago I was going to take a bath in my hotel room after a long day of presenting a workshop. I love a luxurious, hot bath. As I went to step into the water I realized it was tepid rather than hot. I tried turning the hot water spigot on full blast, but the water was cool. In short order I heard myself complaining and immediately stopped in my tracks, realizing I was exhibiting a profound lack of gratitude. I spontaneously said, *"Really? Really!?"* to myself out loud. Clean water is a luxury from a global perspective. Most people in the world don't even have enough water to drink, much less immerse their whole body in as an indulgence. In some cultures the biggest chunk of the day can be finding and transporting water. And here I was complaining that it wasn't the exact temperature to which I felt entitled. I was humbled. I immediately began to express gratitude. As a result, my bathing experience was transformed into one of joy and appreciation. A few days later, I saw a poster that profoundly impacted me. It depicted someone obviously from a poorer nation commenting to someone who was clearly from a richer nation; "So let me get this straight…you have so much water in your country that you poop in it?" Talk about perspective! It was a stark reminder that rooted the lesson from a few days ago even more deeply. Ever since that experience I feel a tremendous sense of gratitude with every shower and bath I am privileged to take.

Gratitude is the fastest path to joy and contentment. Sometimes it is confused with a feeling of indebtedness. But it's not the same thing at all. When you feel indebted you feel a sense of obligation. Feeling indebted fosters feelings of disconnection and guilt, whereas gratefulness nurtures and strengthens relationships.

Some benefits of a grateful attitude include:

Increased happiness: Some studies have shown that long-term feelings of well-being increase significantly when an attitude of gratefulness is nurtured.[7] Gratitude isn't just attitudinal; it profoundly affects you psychologically and physiologically. Increased levels of hormones and neurotransmitters associated with feelings of well-being are experienced when you are grateful. Fewer stress hormones are produced, and therefore fewer feelings of stress are experienced. Your body and brain chemistry actually fuel happiness when you are thankful.

Becoming less materialistic: Materialism tends to foster feelings of dissatisfaction, encourages self-centeredness and is correlated with increased incidence of mental disorders. There is a difference between wanting to enjoy the finer things in life and materialism. Materialism is the desire for more, to the exclusion of appreciating and being grateful for what you already have. Materialism makes you feel inadequate and in a state of constant striving. It prevents you from enjoying the journey. Gratitude, on the other hand, helps you enjoy what you have, even in the midst of preparing to receive and enjoy more in the future.

Better relationships: Gratitude helps you build and strengthen relationships in your life. Adopting a grateful mindset reduces self-centeredness because you are focusing on someone or something outside of yourself for which you are grateful. When you are thankful for what someone has done for you, your focus is on them rather than on yourself. You are thinking about *their* generosity and kindness. When you express that gratitude, you make others feel appreciated and valued.

Greater optimism: Optimism is a natural outgrowth of gratitude. When you are grateful you will more easily see the opportunities imbedded in challenges. Gratitude brings a clarity that promotes a sense of confidence and hopefulness about the future.

Better health: Gratitude has also been linked to a healthier immune system, less stress, less disease and overall better health. People who live with gratitude also have a statistically longer lifespan than those who do not.

Better sleep: Gratitude often reduces insomnia and improves the quality of your sleep. The most significant reason is that a grateful mindset removes, or reduces some of the most significant blocks to sleep – worry, anxiety and feelings of stress. When you are in a state of gratitude you are more relaxed and at ease, which makes it easier to drift off to sleep more quickly.

Increased self-esteem: Living in a state of gratitude includes being grateful for and to yourself. People thrive when they are appreciated. That includes you. When you are grateful to and for yourself, you open the door to more positive self-esteem.

Most of us intuitively know that living in a state of gratitude is a vital ingredient to feeling good, but it can be easy to fall back into discontentment and frustration when things don't go the way you want. But ingratitude can keep you stuck in the very state of unhappiness that you seek to escape. So how can you begin to shift into a grateful paradigm?

Ways to foster gratitude:

Keep a gratitude journal: Studies have shown that people who write down at least 5 things a day for which they are grateful are happier.[8] It takes very little time, and the benefit over time is worth the investment.

Write a thank-you note to someone: Once a week write a thank-you note or email to someone expressing your appreciation for something they have done, or for a way in which they have positively impacted your life. This small gesture will increase your own awareness for what others contribute to your life. It will also help to deepen your relationships with others and make them feel appreciated and loved.

Intentionally search out the positive in every situation: It can be easy to see only the negative in challenging circumstances. But there is always something for which you can be grateful, even if it is the opportunity to learn greater patience or to exercise kindness in the face of adversity. Actively searching for the positive also helps foster a more balanced perspective about what is happening. I love to make this a game. It's fun for me to try to find as many positive things as I can in a difficult situation. This positions you to more easily recognize hidden opportunities might otherwise be missed.

Make a gratitude list: I once listed one thousand things for which I was grateful. The guidelines I set down for this activity were that I couldn't repeat any of the items, and that I would include every aspect of my life that either made my existence possible or enhanced it in some way. I was on number 65 when I realized I had not yet put down "air". Listing the things for which you are grateful can help you to become more mindful of the things you may take for granted on a daily basis.

Chapter 10

Self-Compassion

"If your compassion does not include yourself, it is not complete" Buddha

"Loving yourself is healing the world." Jaymie Gerard

Imagine you are shopping and notice two people in the aisle. One is pushing the shopping cart and the other is walking alongside. Each occasionally stops to compare prices. The person pushing the cart becomes distracted, which results in complete destruction of a carefully built mountain of canned goods. The other person whips around, spitting out, "You idiot! Why didn't you watch where you were going? Can't you ever get anything right? You are so stupid!"

Or imagine a friend who is suffering with chronic low back problems. You witness a mutual acquaintance say to them, "It's your own fault. You never take care of yourself. You deserve it! There is no hope for you because you know you are never going to change!" How would you feel? Would that seem harsh? Would you ever do that to someone? Do you ever do that to *yourself*? What if you treated others the way you treat yourself? Would that be a blessing, or would your family, friends and co-workers have to watch out for periods of insults, nagging, and maybe even emotional abuse?

Self-compassion involves being honest about, and touched by, your own suffering - not avoiding or disconnecting from it. It encompasses the desire to alleviate your suffering and to heal yourself with kindness. Self-compassion also means seeking to understand your pain without judgment or condemnation. It entails seeing your pain, inadequacies and struggles within the larger human experience, rather than getting caught in the self-pitying mindset that you, and you alone, are the only one who suffers. In short, self-compassion is having love and respect for yourself no matter what else you might be experiencing. It makes space for you to be able to be kind to yourself, even in the face of failure, rejection, defeat, or other difficult experiences.

Self-compassion enables you to experience your pain without allowing it to consume you. When you are self-compassionate, you acknowledge your pain and suffering, feel compassion for yourself and seek to take action to alleviate your suffering. It does not avoid or repress, but embraces and comforts. Self-compassion requires mindfulness, and is an essential aspect of emotional maturity.

Self-compassion has three main components: kindness; understanding your experience as part of, and connected to, the larger human experience; and mindfulness. It can be confused with other disempowering qualities. It is, therefore, important to be clear about what self-compassion is not.

Self-compassion is not self-pity. Self-pity contains a "why me?" aspect. It happens when you are immersed in your own pain and difficulties, losing sight of the pain others are experiencing. This tends to result in a lack of compassion for others. It is important to remember that your pain is not unique. Others have experienced problems, failures and suffering similar to yours. When you believe or behave as though you are the only one in the world who is suffering, you reduce your ability to meaningfully connect with others and offer compassion to them in the face of their pain. Self-compassion creates eyes that are able to see that everyone, including you, is deserving of compassion because everyone is interconnected and equal in worth.

Self-compassion does not isolate. It recognizes that feelings of failure and inadequacy are part of the human condition. When you are being self-compassionate you acknowledge that all people, including yourself, are worthy of compassion. Compassion toward yourself is a vital aspect of learning to treat others with compassion because less judgment toward yourself will, over time, lessen your judgment toward others.

Self-compassion is not comparative. It does not ask "Am I good enough?" Self-compassion does not require that you compare yourself to others for evaluation of worth. There are no criteria which you must satisfy in order to show yourself compassion. You are worthy of self-compassion simply because you exist as one part of the inter-connected universe. Self-compassion takes judgment out of the picture.

Self-compassion is not passivity. When you are passive you tend to deny, ignore or neglect the need to take action to rectify a troubling situation. Passivity tends to spring from, as well as foster, victimhood. When you remain passive you give up your power to live into your full potential. Sometimes people are afraid to make a choice, but not making a choice is also a choice. It's a fear-driven choice. When you remain passive you surrender the possibility of making a paradigm shift in your life and circumstance.

Self-compassion is not making excuses. Sometimes people are afraid to let themselves off the hook when they believe they have made a mistake. But self-compassion does not require making excuses for yourself. It's not white-washing, denying or justifying your choice or behavior. It's looking at the situation squarely, without excuses, and forgiving and loving yourself anyway. Self-compassion allows you the emotional freedom to let go of your current disempowering coping strategies and adopt others that are more congruent with how you want to be.

You can't experience personal alchemy without self-compassion Some significant benefits are:

- Less depression and anxiety.

- Transforming suffering and negative moods to more empowered and joyful states.

- Greater knowledge and clarity about your limitations, along with a willingness to honor them.

- The need for perfection is reduced, resulting in a more relaxed state of mind.

- Greater self-knowledge because you aren't hiding your shortcomings from yourself.

- Greater motivation since you aren't immobilized by guilt, but rather are motivated to create change to alleviate suffering and pain.

- More peace. Less stressful thinking results in more peace.

- Greater compassion toward others. When you are compassionate with yourself, you automatically become more compassionate toward others.

How to Foster Self-Compassion:

Notice you are suffering. In order to experience self-compassion you must first notice you are suffering. You may sometimes create so much busyness in your life that you don't even notice you are in distress. You may create busy-ness to avoid your pain as well. Sometimes people immediately turn on the television or radio when they come home so that they don't have to hear their own thoughts. The inability to simply sit in silence can arise from wanting to avoid your thoughts and pain. Sitting in silence is an important way to get in touch with what is happening in your internal environment.

Breathe. When you breathe consciously you are saying "yes" to life. Deliberately regulating your breath is the choice you make to be alive and to connect with yourself and your experience. Breathing settles your body, resulting in a natural reduction of feelings of sadness, anxiety, fatigue, irritation and stress. It can help quiet the chaos of your mind. Take a breath, and instead of repeating self-judging thoughts, breathe in thoughts that engender peace, serenity, and benevolence toward yourself and others. While you breathe watch your thoughts and pain without judgment.

Let go of ego and accept your humanness. Demanding perfection of yourself is a function of ego. We all make mistakes. Realize that your imperfection is a shared human experience. We all experience behaving in ways that are not worthy of us. It's important to have enough humility to simply admit it when you are not where you want to be in a particular area of your life. It's freeing to be able to say, "I didn't handle this the way I wanted, or "I wasn't very kind in that interaction." To accept your personal failing in the moment is a decision of courage, wisdom and humility. I decided years ago that I get to 'suck' sometimes. I'm human. My goal is simply to do whatever I can with quality. Commitment to quality demonstrates integrity. But there is a vast difference between quality and perfectionism. Quality is about integrity, while perfectionism is dysfunctional. I seek to live with integrity and do the most loving, kind and positive thing in a given situation. When I fail to do that, instead of pressuring myself with the guilt of failure, I seek instead to learn from my experience, forgive myself and do it differently next time.

Treat yourself like a friend. Ask yourself, "If I had a friend who was dealing with this, how would I respond?" Then respond to yourself in that way. People often treat themselves in ways that they wouldn't consider treating others. Sometimes they even call themselves names and are verbally abusive with themselves, saying things like, "I'm so stupid!" or "I should know better. What's wrong with me?" Give yourself the same level of compassion and understanding that you would your friend. This may take practice and determination, but it is well worth the focus and attention. Open your heart to yourself in kindness, understanding that you are choosing to feel compassion for yourself, because all human beings deserve compassion and understanding.

Ask yourself, "How can I love myself through this?" This is a powerful question. It can help you get out of self-pity and into active and meaningful self-care. It immediately begins to foster a mindset of self-compassion.

Don't confuse who you are with what you do. You are not your job. You are not your hobby, or your successes or your failures. Sometimes people receive the message while growing up that worth depends on achievement. This is an unfortunate and inaccurate message. You're worth is greater than your best achievement, and not limited by your most spectacular failure. A trite analogy to be sure, but just as the sun may be obscured, but not destroyed by the clouds, so too your actions may temporarily seem to conceal your true essence. Your true self is pure, and inherently of value.

Accept that it may take time for self-compassion to come easily. As the Dalai Lama says, "Cultivating an attitude of compassion and developing wisdom are slow processes. As you gradually internalize techniques for developing morality, concentration of mind, and wisdom, untamed states of mind become less and less frequent. You will need to practice these techniques day by day, year by year. As you transform your mind, you will transform your surroundings. Others will see the benefits of your practice of tolerance and love, and will work at bringing these practices into their own lives."

Self-compassion can help you live in the grace of the moment with acceptance and a sense of peace. I think this poem by Saint Thérèse of Lisieux articulates this so eloquently.

May there be peace within.
May you trust that you are exactly

where you were meant to be.
May you not forget the infinite possibilities
that are born of faith in yourself and others.
May you use the gifts you have received,
and pass on the love
that has been given to you.
May you be content with yourself
just the way you are.
Let this knowledge settle into your bones,
and allow your soul the freedom
to sing, dance, praise, and love.
Life isn't about waiting for the storm to pass.
It's about learning to dance in the rain!

Saint Thérèse of Lisieux

Chapter 11

Embracing Imperfection

"Being happy doesn't mean everything is perfect, it means you have decided to look beyond the imperfections." Unknown

"Ring the bells that still can ring. Forget your perfect offering. There is a crack in everything. That's how the light gets in." Leonard Cohen

Years ago, while attending a three day workshop, I was asked to find something to bring in on the last day that symbolically represented how I see myself. I chose a bonsai tree. I chose it because the beauty of the bonsai tree is in its imperfection. It is perfectly imperfect – or imperfectly perfect. I think the twisting curves and crookedness are actually what makes the bonsai so interesting and appealing. There are no straight, perfect lines; no symmetrical contours - just an unexpected, random meandering form of trunk and branches. I think we are all like the bonsai tree.

You can be imperfect and still be whole. They are not mutually exclusive. My son, Jonathan Gross, states in his book, "The Great Doubt", that possibly the most spiritual thing we can do is to become fully human. I think this is profoundly insightful. The challenge is to accept, and even embrace, the gifts of your imperfections, while at the same time recognizing the incredible beauty that you embody.

What if you accepted yourself exactly as you are? Is that a frightening thought? Do objections immediately rise up within you, like: "But I have a terrible temper!", or "But I'm not very smart!", or "But I am depressed all the time and I hate my life!" I'm not suggesting that you should just lie down and surrender any hope for a more joyful and fulfilling life, or that you shouldn't attempt to heal the emotional triggers that cause you discomfort and pain. I'm proposing that accepting yourself is the key to healing. Accept yourself *even though* you have a terrible temper. Accept yourself *even though* you drink too much. Accept yourself *even though* you are depressed. This is a deep form of self-compassion that allows life-transforming healing to take place.

Many people have grown up with a clear message that anything less than perfect is unacceptable and puts them at risk of being rejected and criticized. Disapproval from the significant people in your life – parents, siblings, teachers, etc. – may have created a strong desire for you to conform to a perceived 'ideal' in order to avoid reprisal from those who had power over you. As a result, imperfection is viewed as something to be feared and hidden.

Imperfection has its gifts. Accepting your imperfections and learning from them can be the doorway to tremendous growth and transformation. It allows the opening necessary to recognize and reap the benefits inherent in your struggles, blemishes and mistakes.

Confusion often occurs when pain and personal identity are viewed as synonymous. However, you are not your anger, depression or frustration. You are not your temper or your addiction. Those are things you feel and experience that arise out of unresolved pain. But those things are not who you are. You are not an amalgamation of your imperfections. In your human, temporal form, you are a synthesis of all your experiences, history, emotional and mental programming, likes, dislikes, hopes, dreams, sorrows, love, failures and successes. Much like the bonsai tree. In a more eternal sense, I propose that you are a part of the divine. You are Spirit.

Gifts of imperfection can help you become a more loving and spiritual being. These gifts can help burn away that which has no value, refining the more precious potential within you.

Benefits of imperfection:

Compassion and Empathy: The gift of imperfection helps to foster a sense of compassion toward others who may be experiencing a similar challenge. It affords you the opportunity to understand and relate to the pain of others. It is much easier to feel compassion toward another person when you have experienced the same situation or made the same mistake. If you have never done something similarly flawed, it can be much more difficult to understand how someone could ever have such a foible. Your own imperfection can assist you in understanding and connecting at a heart level with others. Because of imperfections I have had to wrestle with and overcome in my life as a result of the emotional and sexual abuse I experienced as a child, I now have a deep compassion for and sense of empathy toward people who are experiencing similar struggles. My own struggle to find less destructive ways to cope with my residual pain and scars from my childhood now helps me assist others in their healing as well.

Humility: The gift of imperfection helps you stay humble. Acknowledging my imperfections has created significant discomfort for me at times. I grew up believing that the safest way to control my world was to be perfect, or at least perceived of as perfect by those in authority. I have had to learn to recognize and accept my own humanity, and to embrace the vulnerability that engenders. It can be easy to assume an attitude of superiority when you, or others, see you as perfect. Arrogance and pride create an atmosphere of judgment and separation. Humility is quite relatable. There is something basic and wonderfully child-like about it. A child isn't afraid to admit when they don't know something; or when they can't do something; or if they feel inadequate. There is an authenticity that comes with humility that is disarming and inviting.

Acceptance: The gift of imperfection helps you to accept others in the midst of their imperfections. You are less likely to judge others with harshness when you are dealing with your own failings. I became much more tolerant, for example, of waiting longer than I wanted to in a doctor's office after I started to treat patients myself. I now realize that a variety of things can happen in a day that may interfere with the smooth progression of a schedule. There are times a patient may break down in tears due to a family crisis they are experiencing. It would feel cruel to me to brush them off so that I could stay on time. There are also times when a patient in extreme pain may ask to be squeezed in to my already full schedule. I try to accommodate those types of situations because it seems like the compassionate thing to do. It may also cause me to fall behind in my regularly scheduled appointments. And there are times when, for seemingly no good reason, I simply fall behind. As a result of my inability to perfectly keep my own schedule, I have become much more accepting of being on the receiving end of a schedule mishap.

Depth and Strength of Character: If a tree gets an abundance of water, the roots will be very shallow. If it doesn't get the amount it needs, it will send its roots much deeper into the earth to find water. As a result the tree is stronger. It is also the tree that is most exposed to the buffeting of the wind that is the most resilient. I'm not suggesting that you should purposefully create your own challenges and difficulty so that you will grow stronger, but rather that you use the ample opportunities that will naturally arise during life to deepen and strengthen your purpose and character. Many of these chances for growth will result from facing, accepting, and learning from your own imperfections.

As someone who has experienced sexual, physical, mental and emotional abuse while growing up, I have had a lot of opportunity as an adult to choose the path to growth and healing, or the path of victimhood. At times my choice has been to heal, and at times to remain a victim. But the more often I have chosen to heal, the stronger I have become, and the deeper my emotional roots sink into a foundation of stability.

Catalyst for Transformation: I have much more joy and freedom in my life as a result of dealing with anorexia and Obsessive Compulsive Disorder (OCD) as a young woman. I felt like the most imperfect person on the planet. I was filled with fear, anxiety and self-loathing. Yet, walking through that experience propelled me toward finding a way out of my torment. As a result, I started on the path to self-discovery and personal alchemy. That has allowed me to be where I am today. I am convinced that without the gift of the imperfections of anorexia and OCD I would have settled for a lifetime of feeling deeply unhappy and unfulfilled. Anorexia and OCD were torturous enough to catapult me into making the changes necessary to create more joy and harmony in my life.

Personal Freedom: There is great freedom in relaxing into the awareness that you don't have to be perfect to be enough. This doesn't mean you excuse yourself from living a life of integrity and kindness, or sharing your talents and gifts. It simply means that you loosen your grip on the need for perfection. You allow yourself the grace of self-compassion, especially in the face of your shortcomings and failures. You are benevolent toward yourself at all times, whether you are where you want to be or not. You are willing to give yourself the necessary time to learn and grow. Anxiety and fear lessens when you accept yourself at every phase of your journey, knowing that you are continually moving in the direction of greater freedom, authenticity and personal alchemy.

Chapter 12

Forgiveness

"The weak can never forgive. Forgiveness is the attribute of the strong." Mahatma Gandhi

"Resentment is like drinking poison and then hoping it will kill your enemies." Nelson Mandela

Forgiveness is an essential part of personal alchemy. As Nelson Mandela said in the above quote, "Resentment is like drinking poison and then hoping it will kill your enemies". When you live in a state of unforgiveness you give up varying degrees of your personal power and autonomy. Resentment and bitterness keeps you tied with invisible cords to the very person whom you are loath to forgive.

One thing that can make forgiveness so difficult is confusion about what forgiveness actually means. For example, I remember once hearing someone tell a woman whose body was covered with bruises from the most recent beating from her husband, "Honey, you need to forgive that man and get on back to him!" That certainly doesn't make forgiveness very attractive. Who would even want to consider forgiving if that's what it means? But that's not forgiveness. That's co-dependence masquerading as forgiveness.

It is important to understand what forgiveness is, and is not; what it does and does not ask of the forgiver. It is also vital to differentiate between forgiveness and reconciliation. If the two are confused, it can keep you stuck and tied to the past.

Lack of forgiveness can significantly impact the quality of your life. It can lead to feelings of tension, depression, anxiety, irritability, anger and hurt. It can manifest in your body in a variety of forms, including headaches, neck, shoulder and back pain, digestive distress and insomnia.

Forgiveness only requires one person – you. The person whom you are forgiving does not have to be present, or regretful, or even alive. It requires no contact, relationship or interaction with the person you are forgiving. Indeed, it might not even be safe to have contact with them if there is a history of abuse and violence. But essentially, forgiveness is always in inside job. Reconciliation, on the other hand, requires at least two people; the one forgiving and the one being forgiven. It requires some interaction with the other person. Let me address each one separately.

Forgiveness: Forgiveness is an act of mercy, especially toward yourself. It means letting go of resentment and giving up the 'right' to revenge. It's a gift of peace to yourself. Forgiveness does not condone, excuse or deny what was done. You can still confront whatever injustice you feel you experienced honestly – and choose to forgive anyway.

Forgiving is also not forgetting. Your memory doesn't suddenly go blank simply because you choose to forgive someone. Forgiveness does not remove accountability from the person who you are forgiving. If, for example, they embezzled from your business they may need to be reported to the appropriate authorities. And you can still forgive them. Forgiveness is a decision of strength, not weakness, as Gandhi stated in the quote at the beginning of this chapter. It allows you to begin to heal, and severs the bonds to the past that have kept you stuck. It is letting go of the past so that you may fully embrace the potential of the present and future.

Forgiveness is choosing to no longer let anger and hatred guide your actions, thoughts and life. It is deciding to stop perpetuating your own suffering. Forgiveness is an act of self-love and a choice to live in peace.

Reconciliation: Reconciliation requires that the person who wronged you be remorseful. True reconciliation also requires a demonstration of healthy change. So, for example, an alcoholic spouse might need to remain sober, be in therapy, go to some type of 12 step program, hold a job, and demonstrate other necessary shifts over a significant time period before reconciliation would be possible – assuming it was even desired. It means the person being forgiven must accept accountability for what they have done. Reconciliation does not mean going back to the same old relationship and interactions without change. New conditions, based on a foundation of healthy personal and mutual esteem and respect, must be met. It also demands honest dialogue, with each person acknowledging their own responsibility in whatever occurred.

While you may not always be able to reconcile with another person, you can always find the release that forgiveness offers. Why doesn't everyone choose to release the power that the past holds over them and opt to forgive?

Common reasons people don't forgive:

Personal expectations and definitions: People confuse forgivenes and reconciliation. They think establishing healthy expectations anc boundaries in relationships isn't unconditional love. They believe i someone say's "I'm sorry" that should be the end of the matter. The truth is that often contrition may be just the first step of many in a healthy re-negotiation of the relationship.

Taught and learned responses: People may have learned coping strategies to survive dysfunctional relationships. These can include raging, blaming, clamming up, numbing, disassociating, etc.

Unhealed Wounds: Unresolved pain from the past - such as feelings of abandonment, low self-esteem, anger, fear, feelings of unworthiness, etc. - can create barriers to forgiveness. The path of forgiveness can illuminate areas in which you still need to heal emotionally.

Fear: Fear of making yourself vulnerable can make you push forgiveness away. But true forgiveness actually empowers you to make more centered decisions about healthy boundaries. In releasing the ties that keep you bound to the person whom you feel hurt you, you are able to make choices without the emotional baggage associated with the person.

Two-valued perspective: Sometimes people judge what is right and wrong based on their own experiences, teachings and perspectives. However, things are seldom either/or. Usually there are a variety of ways in which you might be able to view any given situation. A two-valued perspective is limiting and can create feelings of judgment. Trying to see things from the other person's perspective can be helpful in the process of forgiveness. It can provide valuable insight that can help you move in the direction of forgiveness.

Victim mentality: In an unhealthy way, it can feel satisfying to play the victim. It elicits sympathy and empathy from others, and it removes any responsibility from you for your choices and responses that may have contributed or exacerbated the situation. Blaming someone totally for your pain can be a ready excuse to avoid change.

Feeling superior: Feeling superior or better than the other person can block forgiveness. If you believe the other person doesn't deserve it, or that they are inherently less than you because of their actions, then you will likely struggle with forgiveness.

Shame: When someone has hurt you, there may be feelings of shame that you allowed yourself to be so vulnerable. Not wanting to look at, or confront, those feelings of shame can also keep you from looking more deeply at the situation, the need to forgive, and where you may be in the forgiveness process.

Hidden anger: You can't forgive what you don't see. Sometimes people repress feelings of anger as a learned response. You may have been taught as a child that being angry is not safe, or that anger makes you a bad person. But anger is often the emotion that fuels the process that allows you to draw healthy boundaries. Learning to recognize, acknowledge and process angry feelings can be important aspects of forgiving.

The need to be right: It can be easy to maintain your rightness as a reason to hold on to anger. But forgiveness doesn't require that one person must be right and the other be wrong. The decision to forgive transcends issues of who's right and who's wrong. Forgiveness may say, "I feel I have been wronged, but I will forgive anyway."

Deciding the act is unforgiveable: It's important to remember that, although you believe the *act* is unforgiveable, the *person* is not unforgiveable. Henry Wadsworth Longfellow said it well; "If we could read the secret history of our enemies we should find in each man's life sorrow and suffering enough to disarm all hostility."

One of the most powerful examples of forgiveness, at a depth that I can't even begin to fathom, is demonstrated by a poem found on the body of a child in the holocaust when the Allied troops liberated Ravensbruck concentration camp in 1945. Ninety-two thousand women and children lost their lives in the horrific brutality that had been perpetrated on them. It says:

> Oh Lord,
> Remember not only the men and women of goodwill,
> But also those of ill will.
> But do not only remember the suffering they have inflicted on us,
> Remember the fruits we brought thanks to this suffering.

Our comradeship, our loyalty, our humility,
The courage, the generosity,
The greatness of heart which has grown out of all this.
And when they come to judgment,
Let all the fruits that we have borne
Be their forgiveness.
Amen, Amen, Amen.

Most people embrace the concept of forgiveness, but doing the hard work that forgiveness requires isn't easy. Forgiveness is radical. It's an act of courage and strength. It demands and forges exceptional emotional maturity. Forgiveness doesn't mean that atrocious acts *deserve* to be forgiven, but it serves to dissolve your emotional ties to the person or people who caused you harm. Its gift is freedom and healing. It is one of the most powerful tools in the process of personal alchemy.

Chapter 13

The Power of Focus

"Always remember, your focus determines your reality."
Qui-Gon to Anakin, Star Wars

"Drink your tea slowly and reverently, as if it is the axis on which the world earth revolves – slowly, evenly, without rushing toward the future. Live the actual moment." Thich Nhat Hanh

The power of focus allows you to make substantial paradigm shifts over time. When your focus is scattered or undirected it's challenging to create any substantial shift. Focus increases power. Consider the power of harnessing and focusing light. When it is highly focused in a directed and congruent way as a laser beam it can cut steel. Giving one thing your full attention in the present moment taps into the power of focus. When you do this repeatedly over a period of time, you gain understanding about and mastery over that on which you have placed your attention. What you repeatedly focus on gains strength in your brain's neural network. Often the benefit of focus is noticed gradually.

It's important to choose what you focus on judiciously, because what you focus on tends to be what you automatically move toward. As I mentioned in a previous chapter, even though the parachute jump trainees were admonished to avoid the one lone tree in the area when they jumped, almost every jumper slammed into the tree! Why? That was where they focused their attention.

The answer to a problem is never found by focusing on the problem. Focusing on the solution, and what you want to happen, is most beneficial. Focusing on sickness doesn't create good health. Focusing on financial lack doesn't create wealth. Focusing your attention exclusively on a problem just tends to magnify it. That doesn't mean, however, you ignore a problem. You can acknowledge the problem but keep your focus on finding or creating a solution. It also doesn't mean you ignore your emotional response to the problem. You can acknowledge, feel and process your emotions, and still focus on finding or implementing a solution.

To use the principle of focus beneficially, there are several things to keep in mind.

Focus on what you want, not on what you don't want. What yo focus on tends to expand and grow; it's what you will naturally mov toward. If you want to improve your health, then focus on building and maintaining radiant health rather than focusing on your pain or sickness.

Act "as if". Your emotions work backwards too. Just as your emotions can affect your body language and actions, your body language and actions can affect your emotions. Even if you don't feel positive, healthy or strong, acting like you do will elicit chemicals and hormones in your body that support healing and good health. The mind/body connection is a two-way street. Thoughts and emotions can affect the body, but the body can affect thoughts and emotions as well.

Live in the present moment. Don't dwell on painful events from the past or future - that can start a cascade of negative thoughts and painful emotions. The more you can keep your focus on the present moment, the more peaceful you will feel. Whatever you are doing, including mundane tasks like washing the dishes, give it your full attention. Notice the sensation of the water on your hands, the temperature, the wetness, the feel of the dish in your hand... When you stay in the present moment, stressful feelings often begin to subside. Staying in the moment, however, does require a decision to channel your attention and focus on your current experience.

Use Visualization. This is great way to utilize the power of focus. Visualization employs your imagination, rather than your eyes, to create images in your mind. This process creates the same electrical and chemical responses in your brain as the actual experience would produce.

A study conducted by Dr. Judd Blaslotto at the University of Chicago demonstrated the remarkable effectiveness of visualization. Basketball players were divided into three groups. The goal of the experiment was to see which group was most able to improve their foul shots in 30 days. Each group's foul shot skills were assessed prior to the experiment. After ascertaining the level at which each group performed, the groups were given specific instructions. Group A was instructed to practice shooting foul shots an hour each day. Group B was told to not engage in practice physically, but rather to visualize themselves making foul shots. Group C was the control group and was instructed to not practice or visualize practicing. After 30 days each group was tested again for their level of skill shooting foul shots. Group A, who practiced daily, improved by 24%. Group B, who visualized daily – but did not practice, improved by 23%. Group C, who did not practice at all, did not improve at all. This study is one of many that have clearly demonstrated that visualization is almost as effective in improving skills and initiating change as is action. This approach can be used to effect change in any area of your life.

Focus requires some solitude and quietness. Constant noise and distraction weakens your ability to focus. We all need a balance of activity and rest, connection and alone time, noise and silence. Constant noise and activity cuts you off from the ability to hear your own thoughts and access your own internal wisdom.

Chapter 14

Meaningful Stories

"Everything we hear is an opinion not a fact. Everything we see is a perspective not the truth."
Marcus Arelius

"There are no facts, only interpretations." Friedrich Nietzsche

We all tell ourselves stories. It stems from a desire to understand and create closure regarding what we experience in the world. Stories give shape to the myriad events in life that seem chaotic, confusing and disconnected. They help us understand and give meaning to our experiences. They provide a way to integrate what we see, our current paradigms, our feelings, and our logic.

If someone cuts you off in traffic your story might be, "What a jerk! He thinks he owns the road…" Or it might be, "Wow, I wonder if he is on the way to the birth of his first child!" The emotion you experience depends on the story you tell yourself about the experience. The first story creates a sense of irritation, while the second story elicits a feeling of joy and excitement. The interesting thing is that, with both stories, *you are making it up!* I've decided that as long as I am making it up anyway, I'm going to make up a story that either makes me feel good, or elicits compassion for the other person. Why make up a story that makes me feel miserable?

Choosing a best story doesn't mean that you have to ignore the objective reality of whatever is happening. In the above example, you can still acknowledge that the person is not driving safely. You will probably even want to give them a wide berth on the road in order to preserve your own safety. But choosing to tell yourself the best possible story will also ensure that the experience doesn't ruin your mood.

A few years ago when I was visiting New York I was a passenger in a car driven by someone to whom I am very close. Another car abruptly changed lanes, cutting us off as they screeched into a Burger King parking lot. The driver of our car turned to me and said, "Yeah, tell me a good story about *that*…Ohhhh, I just gotta get my burger and fries or I'm gonna die!" I responded that there were many possible stories that could easily explain the driver's behavior. What if the person was diabetic and recognized they needed food immediately to avoid a crisis? Suppose they were on their way to the hospital and had gotten slightly lost? What if they were late for work and had been warned that one more tardy arrival would result in termination? There were many possible stories that allowed me to not judge the person negatively or create stress for myself.

Creating a best story doesn't mean you make yourself a doormat or tolerate abusive behavior. Suppose you are served undercooked poultry in a restaurant, and are treated rudely when you inform the server of that fact. You can recognize the server's unkind response, politely insist on a resolution to your concern, and still create a best story about the server.

Steven Covey told a story in his book, Seven Habits of Highly Effective People, that demonstrates the power of stories and paradigms. He was on a train one day and a man with his two children got on the train. The man sat down and closed his eyes. The children began to run wild, grabbing things from other passengers and stepping all over them in the process. Steven, along with the other passengers found himself getting angrier and angrier, judging the man harshly for his lack of control over his children. Finally, Steven asked the man to please control his children. The man shook himself out of a stupor and told Steven that they were on their way home from the hospital where the children's mother had just died. Steven said that his paradigm instantly changed from one of judgment to one of compassion.

You can't assume to know what might be driving someone's behavior. They could have just had a death in the family; they might be in the middle of a divorce; they might have just learned they have cancer...who knows? I once knew someone whose spouse died, was fired for being gone from work too often while their spouse was in the hospital, and was a victim of identity theft – all in the same week.

Research has shown that your stories impact and help create your neural pathways over time.[9] The more positive the meaning you ascribe to what is occurring, the more the neural pathways fire that support positive emotions. In other words, your stories determine your emotional experience about events. If you tell yourself better stories, then you create a more satisfying emotional experience. The meaning you give to events in your life, as well as the stories you hear from others, influences your level of optimism.

Optimism doesn't mean a state of perpetual naive, oblivious happiness. It also doesn't preclude being in touch with reality. It does mean making space for, and searching for the best possibility. It's giving people and the unfolding of life the benefit of the doubt. Sometimes people are afraid to create meaningful, more positive stories. Assigning positive meaning to a situation can feel risky, and makes you feel mor vulnerable to a possible negative outcome. Even so, embracing th feeling of vulnerability, and creating a meaningful story anyway, can be powerful step toward living a more joyful, hopeful life.

Learning to create meaningful stories requires practice and th willingness to let go of the need to be right about your current, impulsiv story. Recognizing the initial default story as soon as you are aware of i is the first step toward creating a more meaningful story. Challenging the truth of the initial story is the next step. At this point it may become clear that the story actually has no basis in fact. Once you have that awareness, you have the opening to mindfully generate new, equally possible stories. This can be a fun, creative process. I like to see how many possible stories I can make up off the top of my head. As I generate these stories it also reminds me that there are many possible stories I can assign to any event. Even if the objective facts about a situation are clear, the meaning I give to the incident will determine the quality of my experience. The more often I do it, the more often I will be able to see the world around me through a positive filter.

Chapter 15

Surrender and Perseverance

"The man who moves a mountain begins by carrying away small stones." Confucius

"Success is going from failure to failure without loss of enthusiasm."
Winston Churchill

Surrendering and persevering are both vital elements for personal alchemy. You must surrender to your current situation before you can move forward. Perseverance is a necessary ingredient since change often occurs over time.

Surrendering doesn't mean giving up. It means accepting the reality of your current state. Accepting where you are in life is imperative so that you can formulate an effective plan for change. Imagine the futility of plotting a route from Illinois to Florida when you are starting in Maine. Acknowledging your emotional circumstances allows you to have clarity for the path in front of you. Resisting keeps you stuck. As the saying goes, "What you resist persists".

Perseverance is the natural outflow of believing that it is possible to do that which you have undertaken. It may take time, energy, faith and picking yourself up repeatedly, but it involves a decision to continue undeterred on your chosen path.

Many years ago I read a true story about a cross-country skier who had fallen into an underground cavern. He landed in a stream and broke his leg. The cavern was about ten feet deep, with walls that over time had been worn as smooth as glass by the flowing water; there were no handholds to be found. He hadn't told anyone where he was going, so if he was to survive he knew he had to find a way out. The first thing he had to do was accept the seriousness of his plight so that he could devise a plan to get out.

He tied a length of rope around a large rock, and repeatedly threw it out the cavern's opening. He tried thousands of times over multiple days to get the rock to catch on something. His arms felt like lead, his leg was a mess and he was weak from pain and hunger. Twice the rock did catch on something, only to send him plummeting down again when it broke loose. He continued to toss the rock up. Again, and again and again, until his arm felt like it was on fire from the effort.

Finally the rock caught and held. He was able to pull himself up an eventually made it to a hospital. When he was later interviewed I wa deeply moved by his response to the press. He said, "*I just keep thinkin what would have happened if I had tried one less time!*"

Many people find perseverance challenging because of thei dysfunctional relationship with failure. You may have learned that failing in an endeavor means that you, yourself are a failure. However, every failure is a chance to grow, learn and transform your life. There is a saying; "Success comes from experience, and experience comes from failure." What is most important is to learn from the perceived failure so that you can move closer to your desired goal.

Michael Jordan, arguably the best basketball player of all time, credits his stunning success as a player to his many failures. He once said, "I've missed more than 9000 shots in my career. I've lost almost 300 games. 26 times, I've been trusted to take the game winning shot and missed. I've failed over and over and over again in my life. And that is why I succeed." He recognized that it takes practice to build substantial skills, and failure is an inevitable part of building and perfecting talents and potential.

Chris Gardner, whose life inspired the movie "The Pursuit of Happyness", persevered through the grief of his wife leaving him, the loss of his job, and a period of homelessness to become a multi-millionaire and owner of his own investment company.

The only time failure is assured is when you are stuck in resistance or you give up. As long as you are willing to remain open, a shift is always possible. Don't limit yourself or sell yourself short. Sometimes you may need to find a different approach to achieve what you desire, or find alternative ways to deal with personal challenges. But, if you persevere and have enough motivation, there is always a way. Kyle Maynard, born without legs climbed Mt. Kilimanjaro. Beethoven wrote one of the greatest musical scores of all time after becoming deaf. Esref Armagan, blind from birth, is a prolific and talented painter. Stephen Hawking, completely immobile due to advanced cerebral palsy, is arguably the most brilliant scientific mind alive today. And the list could go on. It's important to remind yourself that, when you are faced with an obstacle or hurdle you may simply need to find a way around it. Many others have. You can, too.

Chapter 16

Nutrition for Happy Chemistry

"Chronic disease is a foodborne illness. We ate our way into this mess, and we must eat our way out."
Mark Hyman

"Let food be thy medicine, thy medicine shall be thy food" Hippocrates

If you want to feel joyful, excited about life and happy, you have to give your body the raw materials it needs to make the hormones, enzymes and various chemicals that support those feelings. Emotions are essentially chemical and hormonal interactions. Your body needs a balance of vitamins, minerals, healthy fats, protein, carbohydrates and water in order to feel good. This chapter is intended to help highlight the basics necessary in order to support your brain and body, making personal alchemy possible.

Feeling good physically can contribute to feeling good emotionally. If you constantly struggle with fatigue and/or pain it can be challenging to experience joy, have open-hearted interactions and embrace life. Supporting your physical health nutritionally enables you to more freely move away from a consuming self-focus and be present for yourself and others in ways that bring you joy and satisfaction.

It's important to remember that each individual choice, collectively, creates health or lack of health. It's easy to fool yourself into thinking, "It's just one doughnut." or "I'm just having a handful of chips." or "I just want to stay up one more hour to finish this game..." But it is the cumulative effect of each choice that builds or tears down your health. Your choices either put a brick on the structure of your health...or take a brick off.

One simple guideline to help you begin to fill your kitchen with healthier foods is to primarily shop on the outside edges and aisles of the grocery store. This is where you will find real food that is nutritionally "alive", while the inside aisles of the store will be filled with processed food that lacks any real substance.

The kind of diet that will support you in feeling emotionally and physically healthy is, in my experience, somewhat different than the typical American diet – even one that isn't filled with junk food. The traditional food pyramid recommends the bulk of your food be grain-based foods. After grains, fruits and vegetables should be most consumed, then meat, poultry, fish, eggs, dairy, beans and nuts. The to of the pyramid – to be consumed only sparingly – is fat and oils. Bu there are problems with this type of diet. Excessive consumption o grains, especially those that have been genetically modified, increase inflammation in the body. This can lead to pain, negatively affect the digestive system and exacerbate painful emotional states. Additionally gluten, a major component of many grains, is increasingly being targeted as a contributor to emotional, as well as physical problems. There are a variety of reasons why this is true, but it is believed by many health care practitioners that there is a very real connection between consumption of gluten and anxiety.

For optimal health I recommend vegetables make up the bulk of your diet. They are powerhouses of nutrition, and help keep your body properly alkalinized. A system that is too acidic can't recover from stress. It's important to lightly cook some vegetables in order to fully reap their nutritional benefit. If a vegetable's color becomes more vibrant with cooking (such as broccoli, kale and spinach), then that is a vegetable best eaten cooked. The heat releases the phytonutrients, which is what causes the color of the vegetable to brighten. Vegetables don't need to be boring. Spices can bring a lot of flavor and kick to them. Thinking of vegetables as a 'main dish' may help you to begin to think about how to season them, much like you would a meat-based dish. Many websites offer vegetables recipes that use spices and seasonings to make them tasty and enjoyable.

Lean protein is the next food your body requires in quantity for health. Protein needs vary from person to person, depending on level of activity and physical stress. Good dietary sources of protein include: some vegetables - especially dark green and asparagus, chia seeds, hemp seeds, quinoa, pumpkin seeds, free-range organic eggs, wild-caught fish, organic poultry and lean organic grass-fed beef. I'm generally not a fan of dairy, but if consumed it should be organic and unpasteurized to ensure the enzymes necessary for digestion are still present. Most protein powder is low-quality and lifeless. It also is typically filled with refined and/or artificial sweeteners, chemicals and various forms of monosodium glutamate (MSG). I always suggest opting for real, live food.

Healthy fats and oils are next on the list of my recommended food pyramid. Low-fat diets are not good for you. Your body needs fat in order to make necessary hormones and chemicals in the body, to lubricate joints, to moisten skin, to produce energy and to nourish the brain. Healthy oils are essential to support emotional health. Some good sources of oil include olive oil (which should only be used cold because it has a very low heat tolerance and will transform into a bad fat with high heat), coconut oil, flax oil, fish oil, borage oil, grapeseed oil, hemp oil, and evening primrose oil. Raw nuts and seeds are also rich in healthy oils. Dry roasting nuts destabilizes the oils, so they become rancid very quickly.

The next category on my recommended food pyramid is fruit. Most people consume too much fruit. I recommend only one to two pieces per day. Fruit is higher in natural sugar than vegetables, and excessive consumption can encourage the growth of intestinal candida.

The last part of my food pyramid is grains. These should be consumed sparingly, and only if they are non-GMO (not genetically modified).

In addition to the above considerations, reducing or avoiding sugar can be extremely helpful. Too much sugar can contribute to blood sugar related mood swings and elevate blood acid levels, which contributes to anxiety and panic attacks. Too much caffeine should likewise be avoided. While one or two cups of coffee has been found to have many significant health benefits, excessive caffeine contributes to nervousness, anxiety, fear and can induce heart palpitations.

Start to look at your choices with a long term perspective. Be honest with yourself about the pattern of your choices and the likely outcome if you continue with the same overall approach. Although some people are able and willing to make massive dietary changes overnight, many people find that challenging. If you find changing your diet a daunting task consider this approach. Ask yourself, "What is one food that I like and know would support my health that I would be willing to add to my diet every day this week?" Then decide when during the day you will eat it - otherwise you may forget. Also ask yourself, "What is something I am consuming that I know is harming my health that I would be willing to let go of this week?" For some people that might be letting go of four of their twelve cans of diet soda per day. That counts. The following week you keep the changes you made, and add another food and let go of something else. In this way you can begin to slowly, but surely, transform your diet into a healthier way of eating.

For those of you who are interested in more in-depth information, below is an overview of some of the most important elements your body and brain require to help create and support a life of joy.

Amino Acids: Amino acids are the building blocks of protein. Your body needs an adequate amount of good, lean protein in order to make neurotransmitters, which regulate mood. A balance of various neurotransmitters such as serotonin, dopamine, norepinephrine and GABA are needed for balanced emotional health.

Sometimes you may need to supplement specific, individual amino acids in order to support emotional health. If you have experienced protracted or severe periods of stress in your life, your body may have learned to produce too much of certain neurotransmitters and not enough of others. This is your body's way of trying to help you through times of perceived danger. For example, your body may have learned to produce too much norepinephrine – which helps you remain alert and vigilant, but not enough serotonin – which helps you feel emotionally balanced and calm. This pattern can become habituated over time. Supplementation can assist the body in achieving a healthier state.

The wonderful thing about supplementing with amino acids is that you will know almost right away if it is what you need. One of the best books on this topic is "The Chemistry of Joy" by Henry Emmons. It can help you quickly assess what your particular food and/or supplements needs might be to support a joyful paradigm. Some of the most significant mood neurotransmitters include:

- **Serotonin:** Adequate levels of serotonin are important for experiencing a calm, yet happy mood. It is made from an amino acid called l-tryptophan. Many people associate l-tryptophan with Thanksgiving because it is plentiful in turkey. In addition to making serotonin, l-tryptophan is also converted into melatonin which is essential for restful sleep. Because serotonin promotes a happy, calm, mood, it also helps keep more excitable neurotransmitters in check. A sufficient serotonin level also helps alleviate depression and insomnia.

  In order to ensure that you get adequate levels of tryptophan it is important to include enough protein and complex carbohydrates in your diet – preferably not grains. Many amino acids compete with each other for assimilation. L-tryptophan can lose out unless you are also getting enough complex carbohydrates in your diet. These include yams, sweet potatoes, beans, lentils, etc. The healthy starches.

Foods high in l-tryptophan include nuts and seeds, bananas, legumes, brown rice, oats and dairy, most animal proteins and seafood.

- **Dopamine:** Dopamine acts as both an inhibitory as well as an excitatory neurotransmitter. Dopamine is associated with feelings of pleasure and desire. Sometimes people who find no pleasure in anything may be deficient in dopamine. Too much dopamine, however, can lead to addiction. Low levels of dopamine interferes the ability to focus, while elevated levels cause excessive focus, and a skewed experience of heightened sensations – sometimes leading to feelings of paranoia and suspicion.

    Dopamine is made from the amino acids phenylalanine and tyrosine. Foods that can help your body with dopamine production include apples, bananas, watermelon, leafy green vegetables, beets, spirulina, meat, fish, chocolate, legumes, seeds, wheat germ, eggs, and dairy.

- **Norepinephrine:** Norepinephrine is a wake-up, excitatory neurotransmitter. It can help us feel excited about life, attentive and energetic. Low levels often manifest as lethargy, depression and apathy. Too much can lead to anxiety and hyper-vigilance. Norepinephrine requires adequate dietary tyrosine and phenylalanine. Fruits and vegetables, raw nuts, meat, fish and dairy are major sources of these elements.

- **Glutamate:** Glutamate is a neurotransmitter essential for metabolism and brain function. It is one of the most excitatory neurotransmitters. It is also the most abundant amino acid in protein. Glutamate occurs naturally in protein-containing foods such as cheese, milk, mushrooms, meat, fish, and many vegetables. Although it is not the same as MSG, or monosodium glutamate, which is the *salt* of the glutamate amino acid, if it is consumed in excess it can affect the body in much the same way. Some glutamate may also convert to naturally-formed MSG during the production of highly processed foods. Since glutamate is the most common and plentiful amino acid in protein and in the blood, in my opinion it rarely needs supplementation if you have adequate protein intake. Too much

glutamate, resulting from excessive supplementation, can caus
anxiety, nervousness and excitability.

- **GABA:** GABA, or gamma-amino butyric acid, is an importan
inhibitory neurotransmitter in the brain. It helps balance the
more excitatory neurotransmitters. Low levels can result in
anxiety, restlessness, irritability and insomnia. GABA helps you
feel more relaxed and at ease, as well as helping you sleep better.
It is generally made in abundance in the body. Since several
neurological disorders, such as epilepsy, sleep disorders, and
Parkinson's disease are affected by this neurotransmitter it is
important to be careful in using supplements to enhance GABA
levels in the body. GABA is made in the brain from the amino
acid glutamate with the aid of vitamin B6. Since glutamate is so
prevalent in food and in your body, often if there is a GABA
deficiency, it is due to a diet insufficient in vitamin B6.

Essential Fatty Acids: In addition to adequate levels of amino acids,
essential fatty acids, or EFAs are key to physical, mental and emotional
health. Your brain is approximately two-thirds fat, so if you are not
consuming enough good fats you compromise your emotional and
mental health. Your brain needs EFAs in order to function properly.
Fish oil, flax seed oil, borage oil, evening primrose oil, hemp oil, coconut
oil and other healthy oils, as well as raw nuts and seed, are rich in EFAs.
    You may have heard of the benefits of Omega 3. One of the
best sources is fish oil. While plant-based oils must be converted to a
utilizable form by your body, fish oil needs no such conversion for your
body to use it. Fish oil is a nutritional powerhouse; it nourishes the
brain, protects nerve cell membranes, reduces inflammation in the body
and lowers cholesterol.
    Studies on fish oil and emotions have demonstrated its
effectiveness in treating a wide range of emotional concerns including
depression, anxiety, stress responses and even bi-polar disorder.[10]
    Unless you are allergic to fish, fish oil can be incredibly helpful in
balancing your emotions. If you are on a blood thinner you should talk
with your health care provider to be sure that fish oil is appropriate for
you since it has natural blood thinning properties. I typically recommend
around 4,000 international units of fish oil per day as a basic dosage.
    I also recommend adding other healthy oils and nuts throughout
the day. Most people do not consume nearly enough healthy oils. As a
side note, adding healthy oils generally will not cause weight gain. Often

it will have the opposite effect since it can help reduce the food cravings. Food cravings are often your body's awkward attempt to help itself get a temporary 'fix' to replace what is lacking – EFAs.

Water: Water is a basic human need. Just a minimal amount of dehydration can lead to emotional imbalance, including feelings of stress, mental fatigue and depression. Depending on your lifestyle and activity level, the amount of water you need may vary. Most people need between 6-8 eight-ounce glasses of water per day.

Your cells function and communicate electrically, and water is the best conductor of that electricity. If you become dehydrated your cells, including your brain cells, experience a reduction in their ability to effectively communicate. This can negatively impact emotional, cognitive and physiological functions.

B Vitamins: B vitamins, especially B12, B6 and Folic Acid (vitamin B9), are arguably the most essential for healthy nerve function. Nervous system health is important for calm and steady emotions.

Vitamin B protects your neurons (brain cells) from degeneration by breaking down homocysteine, an amino acid toxic to neurons. It's important to eat vitamin B-rich foods on a daily basis since vitamin B is water soluble and therefore is not stored in the body. The best sources are dark green, leafy vegetables; asparagus; strawberries; beans and legumes; melons; citrus fruit and Brewers yeast. Supplementing B complex is what I usually recommend, although there are times when individual B vitamins are warranted.

Iron: Iron is essential for the production of red blood cells, which carry oxygen to every part of your body. Ample iron is needed for proper body and brain function. Depression and irritability may result from low levels of iron. Iron deficiency, or anemia, has particular impact on women who are still menstruating. Iron deficiency is one of the most common causes of fatigue in young women. When you are fatigued it is very difficult to have the energy needed to support the changes you may want to make.

Some good sources of iron include dark green leafy vegetables, prunes, black strap molasses, red meat (opt for grass-fed, organic since it is high in omega 3s and is heart-healthy), egg yolks, liver and legumes.

Selenium: Selenium is an essential trace mineral. Insufficient intake of selenium can contribute to mood disorders. It also helps to regulate blood sugar levels, which can impact emotional well-being. Brazil nuts, meat, and seafood are rich dietary sources of selenium.

Zinc: Zinc is a mineral that helps regulate mood and greatly impacts your immune system. Nuts, shellfish, legumes, red meat, and oysters are all good sources of zinc.

Probiotics: Digestion is vital for healthy emotions. When the flora in the gut becomes imbalanced, emotional issues often result. Overgrowth of intestinal bacteria and fungi destroy your body's ability to produce serotonin, a neurotransmitter that helps you feel emotionally calm. Ninety to ninety-five percent of serotonin is produced in the digestive system. If the digestive system is impaired, anxiety and/or depression often occur. Probiotics help restore healthy gut flora, which is key to a healthy emotional state.

Chapter 17

The Power of Sleep

"Never go to sleep without a request to your subconscious." – Thomas Edison

"Sleep is the best medicine." Dalai Lama

Intuitively, most people know that insufficient sleep can negatively affect emotions and impair cognitive function. Most emotional processing, as well as physical healing, happens while you sleep. If you are not getting enough sleep, it can profoundly affect your well-being. A study from the University of California, Berkeley, and Harvard Medical School demonstrated that sleep deprivation increases emotional reactivity in the emotional centers of the brain. In fact, Matthew Walker, the director of Berkeley's Sleep and Neuroimaging Laboratory, and the study's senior author, asserts that the emotional centers of the brain become 60% more reactive. Lack of sleep increases levels of depression, anxiety and other emotional and psychiatric problems.

When you don't get enough sleep the amygdala, the part of the brain that alerts the body when there is danger, becomes overly active. The result is an increase in chemicals that activate the fight, flight or freeze reflex. The prefrontal cortex, which is in charge of logical reasoning, becomes less active with sleep deprivation. As a result, it becomes less effective at mitigating the amygdala's excessive emotional reactions.

Another recent study highlighted the role of sleep in clearing toxicity from the brain. The brain is not part of the lymphatic system that helps clean the body from toxic accumulation. It has its own system called the glymphatic system. This system only activates during sleep. If you don't get adequate sleep, toxicity builds up in your brain, affecting your emotions, cognition, and neuro-chemical balance.

Getting enough sleep is important for physical and emotional health, but you can also capitalize on sleep in other ways. Sleep can be a time during which you can address and change some of the subconscious thought patterns that create pain in your life. Taking a few moments prior to sleep to visualize yourself with the kinds of attitudes and emotional states that you desire gives your subconscious something to process throughout the night.

Your subconscious mind is most receptive to new thoughts, ideas and images when you are in a relaxed state. Your brain waves change as you start to relax and drift off to sleep, and you actually enter into a type of hypnotic state. This is a wonderful time to focus on thoughts and images that you want to begin to incorporate and integrate into your life.

Follow these four steps prior to going to sleep to make the shifts in your life that you desire:

1. Close your eyes and make a request to your subconscious mind. Don't give a timeline. It can be something like, "I request more energy in my life."

2. Take a minute or two to visualize yourself experiencing what you requested. So, for example, if you requested more energy, imagine yourself doing the things increased levels of energy would afford.

3. Take a minute or two to experience the feelings that more energy will allow you. Be detailed. Let the feeling flood your body.

4. Let the image and feeling settle, and then go to sleep. Your subconscious will process and integrate it, especially since it was the last input before falling asleep.

In order to ensure a good night's sleep it is important to practice good sleep hygiene. Sleep hygiene is system of healthy sleep habits that support your ability to fall asleep and sleep soundly. Below are some guidelines that can help create a healthy sleep environment and sleep habits.

- Don't do anything in bed other than sleep or to having sex. You want your brain to associate bed with sleep.

- Engage in calming activities prior to bed. Allow yourself to decompress from the day. Be aware there is a difference between passive relaxation (watching TV, computer work, etc.) and active relaxation (meditation, looking at the night sky, restorative yoga, etc.). Active relaxation has been found to be more effective at allowing the body's systems to calm down than passive relaxation. Television and computer work can stimulate brain activity.

- Avoid vigorous exercise within two hours of going to bed. Exercising too close to bedtime can increase wakefulness.

- If you have trouble "turning off your mind," try soaking your feet in very warm water for 15 minutes right before going to bed. In Chinese Medicine it's believed that this helps to bring energy down and out of the head. I have seen this make a real difference for some people.

- Make sure your sleeping environment is comfortable, quiet, dark and at a moderate temperature. If necessary, use a sleep mask to make sure the room is dark enough. Any amount of light can prevent your body from producing adequate levels of melatonin, a hormone necessary to help you sleep.

- Establish a ritual prior to bedtime. This signals your brain to prepare for sleep. This can be as simple as turning off the TV, brushing your teeth, reading something inspirational, and taking five minutes to review the things for which you are grateful.

- If you don't fall asleep within a half hour, get out of bed and do something that doesn't require a lot of light, such as meditating or looking at the night sky until you feel sleepy - then go back to bed.

- Don't *try* to go to sleep. Instead, just allow yourself to daydream. Falling asleep is a natural process. *Trying* to go to sleep actually increases tension, making it more difficult. It's like chasing a butterfly. The more you chase it, the more elusive it becomes.

Chapter 18

Quantum Creation

"The cosmos is within us. We are made of star-stuff. We are a way for the universe to know itself."
Carl Sagan

"The atoms or elementary particles themselves are not real; they form a world of potentialities or possibilities rather than one of things or facts." Werner Heisenberg

Much has been written in the last few decades about the power of thought to manifest health, wealth and anything else you might desire in life. Many of these teachings assert that all you have to do to accomplish this is think only positive thoughts that support your desire, and act and feel as if it were already a reality. Theoretically, if you do this, then what you want will inevitably show up in your life, requiring no substantial effort on your part. This is a misleading half-truth.

The modern version of this teaching is commonly known as the Law of Attraction. I want to lay a foundation, and provide context, for the current understanding of this philosophy.

The idea that thoughts have the power to create and manifest reality started to gain momentum with a now famous scientific experiment called the double-slit experiment. This experiment was first conducted by an English scientist named Thomas Young in the 1800s. He sent a beam of light through a plate in which two slits had been cut. As the light passed through the slits, it produced a pattern on a screen behind the plate that could only happen if the light was functioning as a wave. Up until that time it was believed that light was composed of tiny particles. Later, in 1905, Einstein demonstrated that light can behave like a wave or a particle. In 1961 a German physicist, Claus Jönsson, demonstrated that when electrons passed through two slits, they also produced an interference pattern. This proved that not only does light function like both a wave and a particle, but electrons do as well.

Quantum physics suggest a variety of ideas that seem like a page out of a science fiction novel. These include:

- Subatomic particles can be in more than one place at a time.

- Energy, including things that appear solid, can function as a particle or a wave.

- Subatomic particles can disappear, and then reappear anywhere in space, without traveling through that expanse of space.

- The observer affects the behavior and function of the subatomic particle. The presence of an observer is what determines whether it behaves like a wave or particle. How the observer *thinks* the subatomic particle will behave is the deciding factor.

Why is this relevant? Quantum physics suggests that particles, from which everything in the universe is made, exist in a state of uncertainty. This means they don't actually exist in any specific time or place until they are observed. You influence their behavior with how you think about them, and where you place your focus.

According to quantum physics, everything around you is composed of subatomic particles, or energy. Nothing is truly solid. Metaphysics, a marriage of quantum physics and spirituality, also teaches that thought is energy. This is fairly accurate. Your thoughts can be measured electrically.

It has been said that "thoughts are things". From a quantum creation perspective, you have the power to influence subatomic particles using the power of thought. Since everything is in a state of probability, rather than absolute, you have the ability to influence the outcome. But can you - and you alone - create anything and everything you want in life just by the power of your thoughts?

According to Quantum Physics, everything in the universe vibrates at a subatomic level. This impacts the state in which something appears. For example, how fast the atoms and molecules vibrate in water dictates whether it is in a liquid, solid or gas state. Thoughts also have a vibration. This is significant from a metaphysical perspective because thought vibrations are believed to attract similar vibrations. So if your thoughts are of lack, ill health and resentment, then those are the kinds of experiences you will most likely draw into your life. If your thoughts are of abundance, health and forgiveness, then likewise those are the experiences you will manifest in your life. Sounds simple, right? This is where the danger of a half-truth becomes relevant.

Your thoughts *can* influence and play an important role in the creation reality. However, I have also seen this belief system used as a bludgeon of blame. I have had patients, dying of cancer who berate themselves because they haven't been able to reverse their cancer with their thoughts. They can't understand why, if they created it with their thoughts, they can't seem to heal it with their thoughts. And what about the child who was raped at age 14? Did they cause it? What about someone dealing with the loss of a limb from the Boston Marathon bombing? Did they manifest it? I think to suggest so could be taking a more fundamentalist, and dangerous, approach to the understanding of the power to create reality by thought.

The Law of Attraction is not the only law of quantum physics or metaphysics. Just as gravity doesn't function independently of other physical laws, neither does the Law of Attraction. When people are taught the Law of Attraction in isolation it can contribute to feelings of frustration and guilt if it doesn't work. If you say daily affirmations, focus on positive thoughts, do regular visualizations and immerse yourself in the feeling of what it would be like to have what you desire - and yet nothing happens - it can be discouraging to say the least. It can make you wonder if something is fundamentally wrong with you.

The Law of Attraction is not a true law in the strictest sense of the word. A natural law is something that works every time, without exception, as long as the right conditions exist. According to the Law of Attraction, the people, events and situations that show up in a person's life were drawn to them as a result of their own thoughts, attitudes and emotions. Positive thoughts and emotions should always attract positive results. Negative thoughts and emotions should always attract negative results. But it doesn't always work that way.

Two examples that demonstrate that the Law of Attraction is not a true law are Gandhi and Martin Luther King Jr. Both were strong advocates of peace and love, even in the face of hatred, yet each died a violent death at the hand of an assassin. If the Law of Attraction had been a true law, that never should have happened. A better term would be the Principle of Attraction. It is true that positive thoughts and emotions will tend to attract positive experiences, while negative ones will often produce negative experiences. However, there are other important factors that come into play.

Some other principles that are as influential as, and must work in conjunction with The Principle of Attraction include:

The Principle of Oneness: This principle states that we are all connected to everybody and everything in the Universe. This is also a basic tenant of quantum physics. Though it may appear otherwise, from a quantum perspective there is actually no way to scientifically differentiate where I end and you begin. This is one of the principles that helps bring relief to the Principle of Attraction. People sometimes act as if each individual lives in some type of metaphysical bubble; insulated from other people and other forces in the universe. However, each of us is profoundly affected by others, and the choices that we each make individually and collectively. *Together* we have created pollution, war, poverty and weather changes. Those things have an impact. Sometimes the imbalances of the world in which you live may challenge your most positive efforts. For example, if someone gets a form of cancer caused by environmental toxicity due to unethical corporate disposal practices, they cannot be fairly blamed for the illness. While positive thinking and visualization exercises for healing might be helpful, it would be lacking in compassion to lay blame at their feet if they fail to "attract health". We live in relationship. That should not be minimized or dismissed. The world, and its impact on those living in it, is something we create together.

The Principle of Congruency: Your thoughts, beliefs and feelings must be congruent in order to attract what you want. If one of those elements is not aligned with the others, then the Principle of Attraction will not work as you might hope. Difficulty manifesting is often a result of disparate beliefs. These must be identified and changed to align with what you want.

The Principle of Giving and Receiving: You receive back whatever you give. If you are kind, generous and grateful, then you will receive those things from others in your life as well. It may not be in the same form, but it will return to you. One mistake often made in seeking to manifest is a hyper-focus on one's self. If you are constantly in a "gimme" attitude, then you will likely encounter "gimme" attitudes directed toward you. If you nurture an attitude of service and giving, then you will find yourself the beneficiary of generosity in return.

The Principle of Vibration: This principle states that everything is energy and all energy vibrates at various frequencies. Your vibration must match the vibration of that which you hope to attract. Your immediate vibration may change from moment to moment depending on how you are thinking and feeling. However, you do have a basic, core vibrational frequency that has become habituated. This core vibration is what needs to shift over time to match that which you desire. For example, if your core vibration is one of jealously or lack, it must change before you can attract abundance. Feeling abundant will attract abundance. Trying to get wealthier is actually coming from a vibration of lack. The focus is on not being wealthy enough.

The Principle of Gratitude: When you are grateful everything in the Universe conspires to bless you. When you take what you have for granted it cuts off flow.

The Principle of Circulation: There is a season for each thing that comes into your life. There is also a time to release what you no longer need, or no longer serves you. Sometimes letting go is necessary to make room for something better. All energy needs to move and circulate. It's like breathing. If you don't release the last breath you took in, you can't take in the next one to replenish your body with needed oxygen. Holding on, accumulating and hoarding all cause energy to stagnate. Releasing things when you no longer have a need for them provides an opening for other things you might currently be able to utilize. Whatever you want, you must give. If you want money, you need to share money with others. If you want more joy in life, you need to bring joy into the lives of others. Whatever you feel you lack is what you most need to give.

The Principle of Resistance: This principle states that whatever you resist gains traction in your life. Newtonian physics states, "For every action there is an equal and opposite reaction. When you resist something, you initiate a reciprocating force. If you push against the wall, though it might not seem so, the wall is actually pushing back at you. That's a law of physics. Another way to say it is, "Whatever you resist, persists."

The Principle of Appropriate Action: You can think all the positive thoughts you want, but if you are unwilling to take appropriate action when the time is right, you will not succeed. Appropriate action generates and sustains energy. It helps build the momentum necessary to increase the vibration necessary to manifest and create what you want.

The Principle of Change: Everything is always changing. And yet there is nothing new under the sun. A paradox. Even your current life situation is a result of change over time. Your present life is a residual of all your past thoughts, actions and beliefs. That too will change. At times you may find yourself trying to avoid change in your life for fear you will have to surrender your desires. But you can't hold on to anything forever. It's important to embrace and be willing to flow with change. There is a time to receive, and there is a time to let go. Don't fall into the trap of believing that you can attract anything into your life that will be constant and unchanging.

The Principle of Duality: In Chinese Medicine we call it yin and yang. The entire universe is composed of yin and yang energy. There is day - and night; light and darkness; heat and cold; joy and sadness. Everything balances and gives perspective to the other. None of it is bad, it is simply life.

All of the various principles are essential for personal alchemy. Each one is an important piece of the puzzle. Each one helps balance and sustain the others. It's important to remember that you are always manifesting and creating your life through your thoughts, your intentions, your focus and your actions. You either do so by default, or on purpose. Having a daily practice during which you can focus your attention on what you want to create in your life can help ensure that you bring intention to what you are helping co-create.

Chapter 19

Neuro-energetics

"EFT offers great healing benefits." Deepak Chopra, MD

"Treating humans without the concept of energy is treating dead matter!"
Dr. Albert Szent-Gyorgi

There are a variety of powerful, energy and brain entrainment technologies, some of which can be utilized at home. These can help you make the shifts you want to make more easily and more quickly than ever before. Some of these techniques are beginning to gain recognition in the mental health community because of their effectiveness and rapid results. I have successfully used every method I have included in this chapter, and wholeheartedly endorse them all.

Acupuncture and acupressure: Acupuncture is an ancient healing practice. Thought by some authorities to be as much as four thousand years old, it is documented to have been in use for at least two thousand years. Acupuncture helps balance the energy, or Qi (life-force) of the body and promote healing. Just as the body has a circulatory system for the blood, so too, it has a circulatory system for the body's Qi. In Chinese Medicine, the pathways through which the Qi flows are called meridians. When there is imbalance in the flow, quality or strength of the Qi, then symptoms may result. In the case of chronic emotional disharmony, the Qi may be "stuck", deficient or in excess within certain meridians. Acupuncture can help to release, strengthen and harmonize the Qi, resulting in more balanced emotional states.

Acupuncture involves the insertion of extremely fine needles into specific points on the body. The acupoints used depend on the specific needs and diagnosis for each individual, as determined by the treating practitioner. The sensation of the needles upon insertion is nothing like getting a shot. Most of the time there is little to no discomfort involved.

While the exact mechanism of how acupuncture works is still not easily explained, current research has demonstrated its effectiveness.[11] Its ability to bring balance can also have a significant positive impact on emotional health.[12] As a practitioner of Chinese Medicine I have seen and experienced tremendous emotional healing as a result of regular acupuncture treatments.

Traditional acupuncture obviously can't be practiced at home, but it can assist and support the emotional alchemy process. Acupressure can also be a helpful addition to your self-care at home. One exceptional book on the topic is *Acupressure for Emotional Healing: A Self-Care Guide for Trauma, Stress, & Common Emotional Imbalances* by Michael Reed Gach.

Tapping: Tapping is based on the Chinese meridian system of acupuncture. It involves tapping on specific acupuncture points in order to access and clear stuck emotions. Chinese Medicine asserts that there are no bad emotions. Every emotion has a purpose. It's only when emotions get stuck in the body that they create problems.

Emotions are not just feelings. When you experience an emotion, it involves a complex interaction of all the systems in your body - muscular, electrical, circulatory, hormonal, respiratory, cellular and nervous, etc. Whenever you experience a traumatic or stressful event, these systems activate and respond. If the event is traumatic enough, or lasts for a long period of time, the stressful patterns can become habituated and memorized by the body's various systems. As a result the emotion can become lodged in the body. Tapping is a fast and easy way to clear, calm and rebalance these systems.

When I used to teach tapping workshops, I often brought a live tarantula to the class. After tapping, anyone in the class, even those with a lifetime phobia of spiders and arachnids, could fearlessly pet the tarantula after only a few minutes. That's how fast and powerful tapping can be.

Tapping can not only help balance and relieve emotional stress, but can often help improve your health. Stressful feelings are often the root of, or contributors to, many health concerns. Since tapping can reduce or eliminate the emotional distress associated with an illness or pain syndrome, there is often dramatic improvement in physical symptoms as well.

There are a number of variations of Tapping. Some of them include:

- **Thought Field Therapy (TFT):** TFT was the first modern tapping technique, created by an American psychologist named Roger Callahan. This version is very specific and has targeted "recipes" for various emotional issues. It can be a challenge to navigate for people who are not experienced at identifying and working with their own emotional issues. It can be helpful for those with more tapping experience who are seeking to fine-tune their practice.

- **Emotional Freedom Technique (EFT):** EFT, developed by Gary Craig, is probably the most well-known and simplest form of tapping today. It is much easier to use than TFT because the same basic tapping procedure is used for everything. TFT is more akin to diagnosing and fixing a specific part of an engine when a car is malfunctioning. EFT is more like overhauling the entire engine instead of going through each and every part to find the specific problem. EFT helps to rebalance the body's energy flow and the physiological systems associated with the emotional issue. These effects are brought about by bringing attention to the emotional disturbance while tapping on specific points. This process helps dissipate the stuck emotion.

    EFT is a type of energy psychology, or energy medicine. The techniques are easy to learn and very effective. You can find more information and a free, basic tutorial on www.emofree.com.

- **Matrix Reimprinting:** Matrix Reimprinting is a form of EFT. It is extremely helpful for healing emotional pain from childhood trauma. Like TFT and EFT, it helps clear painful emotions and negative, habituated thought systems. It also utilizes the Chinese Medicine meridian system associated with acupuncture. What's different about Matrix Reimprinting is that it involves going back in your memory to help your younger self through the difficult event. You overlay tapping on your own body with imagining tapping on the image of your younger self in your mind – as though the current version of yourself is there to tap on, and assist, the younger self through the challenging event. The goal is to change any negative learning into a positive, healthier learning. This releases blockages at their origin, and helps imprint healthier responses and emotions surrounding painful memories.

The Emotion Code:
The Emotion Code technique is a fast and easy way to clear stuck, uncomfortable emotions from the body's energy system. While there are twelve primary meridians in Chinese Medicine, there are eight others called extraordinary meridians. French acupuncturists sometimes call these "miraculous" meridians because they

can effect therapeutic changes when all other treatment modalities have failed.

The eight extraordinary meridians have some unique functions, one of which is absorbing and storing excess Qi from other meridians. Ideally this stored Qi is made available later should a primary meridian become deficient.

One of the extraordinary meridians is called the governing channel, or DuMai. The DuMai runs vertically along the spine and significantly impacts the entire nervous and energetic systems of the body. Theoretically, the DuMai can absorb and store unprocessed emotions in the form of energy. Clearing this meridian can help release uncomfortably stuck emotions.

The body is electromagnetic in nature. The Emotion Code presents a simple technique for identifying which emotions need to be discharged, along with instructions for using a magnet to release and clear them. Information on The Emotion Code is included in the Additional Reading section.

Neuro-linguistic Programming (NLP): Another technique that can help you make emotional shifts quickly is Neuro-linguistic Programming (NLP). NLP was developed in the 1970s by Richard Bandler and John Grinder. It utilizes the connection between your body's neurological processes (neuro), language (linguistic) and learned behavior (programming) to help facilitate desired change. NLP has been used by individuals and businesses successfully for many years.

While there are a variety of techniques that may be employed with NLP, I want to focus on a specific NLP-based strategy that I have used and found very helpful. It involves a combination of visualization, creativity, accessing past memory and/or fear of the future, and the five senses. It's creative and can even be fun! My suggested process is as follows:

- **Preparation:** Choose a time and place where you won't be interrupted. Turn off the phone. Sit comfortably. Close your eyes. Focus your attention on your breath; just observe it for a few moments. Relax your tongue and bring it softly down to lie at the bottom of your mouth. Imagine there is a sense of increased space around your entire body. Do a slow scan of your body, starting from your feet and moving to the top of your head. If you come across any tension, simply release it as much or as little as it is ready for - and then move on. When you are finished, bring your attention back to your breath. If you are breathing with your chest, move your breath gently down into your abdomen. Sit for a few minutes and just notice.

- **Access the memory or fear of future:** Bring a picture to your mind of whatever memory or future fear you want to address. Make it as vivid as you possibly can. In your mind's eye see the scene as clearly as possible. What colors do you see? Are there people? What position are they in? What size are they? What are they wearing? Is it inside or outside? What sounds do you hear? How loud or soft are the sounds. What tone of voice are people using? Do you feel any sensation on your skin? Are you standing or sitting? Feel the chair or floor beneath your feet. If you are outside and the sun is shining, feel its warmth. Are there any smells? Do you feel any emotions? Be specific. Anger? Happiness? Frustration? Sadness? Fear? Allow yourself to experience it. If you are focusing on a fear of something in the future, allow your imagination to guide you.

- **Make the Change:** Now that you have the memory or fear clearly in your mind, you have the opportunity to play with, and forever change your experience of it. For the sake of clarity I want to share with you a memory that I worked with using NLP. The changes I made during just one session forever altered my relationship with what happened, as well as the memory. This is the original memory:

*Note: This next part may be disturbing to read. It graphically describes a memory of a vicious beating I received when I was a teenager. It is not intended for shock value, but to demonstrate how an intense and painful memory can be altered with utilizing NLP.

When I was 14 years old I received a particularly violent beating from a stepfather. My infraction? I had left a glass of water on the table. He was a big man - and strong. I was 5'3" tall to his 6'4". He beat me with a belt until I had welts all over my back, arms and legs. He was wearing a green shirt. He had a mustache. When it began, we were standing in the kitchen, but as the beating progressed we somehow ended up in the dining room. The sound of the belt as it cut through my skin sounded thunderous to my ears. And the pain of each blow took my breath away with the intensity. His expression was wild, and yet his mouth curved slightly in what appeared to be enjoyment. I was screaming, "Please stop, I won't do it again...I promise!" He just grunted with the effort of the beating. I don't remember any smells. I felt like a wild, wounded and crazed animal just trying to escape, but unable to do so. I even tried climbing the wall to get away. I experienced an unreasonable fear that he would never stop. When he was finished, rage rushed in to replace the terror I had been feeling just a moment before. I had the audacity to clamp my teeth tightly and clench my fists in an attempt to quell the rage inside me. When he saw my expression he beat me again. This time so hard that the next day the school called the police because of the bruises they saw.

This was the NLP process with which I changed my experience of the memory:

After I completed my preparation, I began to change the memory using NLP. I immediately changed the color of everything in the room to grey, including his shirt. When the color was muted, I changed the sound of his grunt to a duck's honk. That seemed humorous to me. I felt inspired. I then shrunk him down to the size of Jiminy Cricket. I noticed right away that the severity of the blows lessened because he was so small. I changed his mustache to a feather that fluttered every time he breathed. That looked ridiculous to me. Then I changed the belt to a wet, cooked strand of spaghetti. Every time he hit me with it, it just kind of fell into pieces and drooped uselessly. It felt like my body had become impervious. Instead of trying to climb the walls, I imagined myself lifting off the floor and flying effortlessly around the room. I felt elated and completely free. Then I changed my response. Instead of begging him to stop, I landed back on the floor, looked him square in the face and said, "You will never touch me again or I will call the police, write the newspaper, call radio and TV stations, as well as your commanding officer and tell them all what you are doing. Someone will listen to me!" I felt empowered and strong as I imagined and felt the words coming out of my mouth. He responded with, "Okay", but in the voice of Donald Duck. I then took the entire scene, shrunk it all down to the size of a postage stamp, and imagined it moving away from me. It got smaller and smaller, until it simply disappeared from sight.

Afterward it became impossible to think of the memory without it being entangled with the changes I had made using NLP. I still know what happened, and can even relate the events as they occurred. However, that is no longer my experience of it. When I think of what happened, I can't separate it from the Donald Duck voice, the wet noodle, the flying around the room, and feeling empowered. The fear and emotional horror is no longer present. Below are suggestions for how to make those kinds of changes using NLP principles.

Changing the Sense of Vision:

- Mute the colors.
- Create static in the scene, like "snow" on a TV screen.
- Make any threatening things/people smaller.
- Change the shape or nature of anything you want.
- Move things further away from you.
- Make whatever you want to experience or keep as part of the memory, more vivid, larger in size and nearer to you.

Changing the Sense of Hearing:

- Make threatening sounds funny.
- Use cartoon character voices.
- Imagine hearing or saying what you want.
- Imagine hearing the comforting voice of your higher power.
- Hear the encouraging voice of your adult self.
- Bring inspiring or funny music into the scenario.

Changing the Sense of Smell:

- Bring your favorite smell into the scene.
- Turn images into a wonderfully smelling vapor.
- See everyone get distracted by a great smell.

Changing the Sense of Touch:

- Change the texture of threatening things to soft or fun textures.
- Change the feeling of pain to that of a feathery tickle.
- Imagine the feel of warm sunshine on your face.
- Imagine the scene goes on "pause", and someone you love comes and gives you a big hug. Feel their arms around you.

Changing the Sense of Taste:

- Imagine the taste of your favorite food in your mouth.
- Imagine you can draw the scene in through a special funnel that converts everything to a delicious flavor. Taste it in your mouth.

Just doing this kind of activity a few times for a particular memory or fear can make a profound difference. Why? It changes your subjective experience of the event. That changes the neuro-pathways on which the memory is carried. This process positively impacts bio-chemical, energetic, hormonal, muscular, cellular, circulatory and respiratory systems in your body.

One note of caution: I have seen people use this technique in a way that I believe isn't helpful in the long run. For example, someone I know was taught to shrink her former abuser down to the size of a cockroach, and then bury him alive to suffer forever. I think it is energetically more advantageous to stick to images that are free from a spirit of vindictiveness.

Brain Entrainment: Another extraordinary tool in using the principle of alchemy for emotional transformation is brain entrainment Brain entrainment has actually been utilized for thousands of years in a variety of indigenous cultures. They have employed drums, chanting, dancing, fasting and flickering firelight to affect and alter brain wave patterns. When the brain is exposed to a rhythmic sound, like the beat of a drum, for example, after a while its electrical impulses begin to synchronize with that rhythm. Historically, various societies have used this method to achieve higher states of consciousness.

Changes in brainwaves occur naturally to everyone, many times during the day. Different brainwaves are associated with sleep, wakefulness, concentration, creativity, feelings of peace, anxiety, etc. There is nothing peculiar about changing brainwaves.

Modern technology has now made it possible to identify and fine-tune the rhythms, pulses and frequencies that produce specific brainwave patterns. Through the use of binaural, monaural and isochronic tones, programs have been developed that help people target specific concerns. So, for example, someone with insomnia might benefit from a brain entrainment program that helps induce sleep brainwaves. Someone with chronic anxiety might find help with a program that helps entrain the brainwaves to a calmer pattern. There are currently scores of programs and systems from which to choose.

One significant impact of brainwave entrainment is hemispheric synchronization – synchronizing the left and right halves of the brain. This is extremely important since people with greater left/right brain synchronization are typically happier, more optimistic and have greater emotional stability.

It might be helpful to know a little about the nature of brainwaves and their impact on your life. For our purposes, I will only deal with four core brainwave states:

- **Beta:** Beta brainwaves occur when you are fully awake and alert. Beta is often associated with intense states of concentrated focus involving cognitive thinking and processing.

- **Alpha:** Alpha brainwaves occur when you are more relaxed. Daydreaming may happen when in alpha state. People often enter alpha brainwaves while watching television. Alpha is the state in which you begin to be more susceptible to suggestions, and the state required for hypnosis.

- **Theta:** Theta brainwaves occur when you are deeply relaxed. This state helps access creative energy, and is associated with a deeper level of subconsciousness. Dreaming occurs in theta. Time spent in theta can help you begin to connect with your own inner wisdom.

- **Delta:** Delta brainwaves occur during deeper sleep. It is a dreamless state in which no thought occurs. It is connected with the unconscious or superconscious state that is thought to provide access to non-physical states of existence. This is also the state in which your body does the most healing.

Using brainwave entrainment with a meditative practice can help you learn to remain conscious as you go progressively into deeper and deeper states. Regularly accessing these deeper states of consciousness, while you remain aware, helps set the stage for permanent changes in the brain, neuro-chemistry and mood.

Subliminal Computer Software: The first few years of your life were spent mostly in theta and delta brainwave states. Initially, everything you learned went straight into your subconscious mind. This is what allowed you to be able to take in such massive amounts of information, and learn so much in a relatively short period of time. It also means that, although you learned a tremendous amount that has made it possible for you to function well in life, you likely also learned a lot that isn't helpful to you. As you became older you were additionally influenced by things you heard and were taught by the significant people in your life, and by society at large. You readily accepted them without judgment since they came from sources you trusted and relied on for survival.

The conscious mind is the logical, rational mind. It asks questions, analyzes, problem solves and stores short term information. As you grow older, and frequently function in beta brainwave state, it also acts as a gatekeeper for the subconscious mind. It decides what ideas, thoughts and suggestions are worthy to allow past. The subconscious mind houses information, beliefs and habits garnered from everything you have ever experienced. If you struggle unsuccessfully to change a habit, mindset or problem, the reason may be that your subconscious mind is operating on an old belief.

Changing unconscious, entrenched beliefs that you learned as a child can be challenging. Bypassing the conscious gatekeeper is often imperative. If, for example, you want to feel happier, but struggle with depression, your conscious mind will filter out efforts to convince yourself that you are happy. It analyzes the idea that you are happy and finds it false. It tosses the thought into the figurative garbage bin. The only answer is to bypass the conscious mind and its judgments. Using subliminal technologies can help a great deal.

The effectiveness of subliminal messages to affect behavior and choices has been recognized and exploited by advertising companies for years. Subliminal messages imbedded in advertisements were used at one time in movie theatres because of how effective they were at bypassing the analytical, conscious mind. The subliminal suggestions to buy snacks went straight into the subconscious mind, resulting in masses of people heading to the concession stand to buy popcorn, candy and soda. This level of mind manipulation was deemed unethical and outlawed.

While I don't endorse or support the use of subliminal messages to manipulate people, I do think there is tremendous value in utilizing them for your own personal growth and transformation. I have used them successfully for years, and have found they are a powerful part of a comprehensive approach to personal alchemy.

I use a program called "Subliminal Power". I choose the ideas, beliefs and affirmations I want my subconscious to accept. I then type those into the software, set the frequency I want the messages to show up on my computer screen and how visible I want the messages to be. I can set them to be completely visible, or barely discernable. In this way, my subconscious mind is being reprogrammed with new, more empowered paradigms while I am working on my computer. Their website address is www.subliminal-power.com (Disclaimer: I am in no way affiliated with the company).

Chapter 20

Life Purpose

"The purpose of life is to live it, to taste experience to the utmost, to reach out eagerly and without fear for newer and richer experience." Eleanor Roosevelt

"The purpose of life is not to be happy. It is to be useful, to be honorable, to be compassionate, to have it make some difference that you have lived and lived well." Ralph Waldo Emerson

Having a life purpose can give your life a sense of meaning. It can provide the impetus to get out of bed in the morning, as well as add excitement and joy to your life. My life purpose is to continue to learn and grow in joy, and share what I have learned with others to assist them in doing the same. This provides me with a frame and context into which everything fits. It helps me to see my life within a larger perspective than just what is happening in the moment. There is a story that demonstrates this concept perfectly.

A man came across three masons who were working at chipping chunks of granite from large blocks. The first seemed unhappy at his job, chipping away and frequently looking at his watch. When the man asked what it was that he was doing, the first mason responded, rather curtly, "I'm hammering this stupid rock, and I can't wait 'til 5:00 when I can go home."

A second mason, seemingly more interested in his work, was hammering diligently and when asked what it was that he was doing, answered, "Well, I'm molding this block of rock so that it can be used with others to construct a wall. It's not bad work, but I'll sure be glad when it's done."

A third mason was hammering at his block fervently, taking time to stand back and admire his work. He chipped off small pieces until he was satisfied that it was the best he could do. When he was questioned about his work he stopped, gazed skyward and proudly proclaimed, "I...am building a cathedral!"

Three men, three different attitudes, all doing the same job.   Author Unknown

The third individual was able to perceive his actions within a much greater context. This enabled him to find satisfaction and joy in

117

the seemingly mundane task of hammering and chipping rocks. So too i is with each of us. If you are able to find meaning in things you do, thei your life takes on depth, richness and focus.

Remind yourself often to stop isolating incidents and look at the bigger picture. This can be an important part of keeping a healthy life perspective. A restaurant server doesn't just serve food, but helps to nourish people so they can give their contributions to others in the community. A delivery truck driver doesn't just drive around and deliver packages, they help people stay connected and feel supported and loved. A refuse worker doesn't just collect garbage; they help keep the community clean, safe and disease-free. A teacher doesn't just teach curriculum, they help nurture minds, develop talents and assist children in becoming the best they can be in life. They lay the groundwork for our society. Whatever you do in your profession or life, find the greater meaning. As a result, you will find a greater sense of satisfaction in the things you do.

You must find and create purpose for your life. I suggest that you not wait for your life purpose to be revealed to you in some mystical way. Each person is endowed with their own unique gifts and talents. Your life purpose will naturally unfold if you pursue your passion and develop your gifts as much as you can. Your interests, and the things that excite you, can clarify ways in which you can contribute to enriching and deepening the lives of others. Don't wait for some transcendent life purpose to hit you like a bolt of lightning. Use and hone your aptitudes and abilities and the way will become clear.

Chapter 21

Empowering Questions

"Successful people ask better questions, and as a result, they get better answers." Tony Robbins

"We thought that we had the answers, it was the questions we had wrong." Bono

The quality of your questions can keep you stuck in pain, or assist you in moving forward. For example, there is a world of difference between the question, "Why me?" and "Now that this has happened, what is the next best step?" One question prevents you from moving forward, while the other opens the way to healing and growth.

The kinds of questions you ask yourself significantly impact your life. They affect your mental attitude and your emotional experiences. They set the stage for everything that follows after the question. If you consistently ask yourself disempowering questions, then you will foster thoughts and feelings of hopelessness, lack, fear and anger. If you ask yourself empowering questions, you will foster thoughts and feelings of worth, hope, joy and peace.

Asking helpful questions can create a powerful shift in your life if you make a regular practice of it. By consistently asking these types of questions, you will begin to change the way you think and approach your life. It will enable you think about your life and circumstances in ways that allow you to see the most positive and beneficial choices.

When I first began on my healing path, I had to change the nature of my questions. Up until then my questions had kept me enmeshed in victimhood. My questions typically were, "Why me?" "Why did this have to happen to me?" and "Why do I have to be the one to do all of this work because someone abused me?" All of these questions kept me stuck because they had no answer. I finally realized that I needed to ask myself different questions if I wanted to make a shift. I started to change my inner dialogue to things like, "It happened. What do I need to heal?"; "How can I love myself through this?"; and "In what ways has what happened made me a stronger, more compassionate and loving person?". These questions began to inform and transform my life in extraordinary ways.

Disempowering questions:

- "Why me?"

- "Why can't I ever get this right?"

- "What's wrong with me?"

- "Why am I so fat...or sick...or unhappy...?"

- "Why does this always happen to me?"

- "Why is my life always so lousy?"

Empowering Questions:

- When I am faced with a particularly difficult situation that I find myself feeling stressed about: *"What would I have to know and what would I have to believe in order to be at peace with this?"*

- When I am sick, feeling overwhelmed or in emotional pain: *"How can I love myself through this?"*

- When I am faced with a task that feels unpleasant, overwhelming or plain distasteful: *"What would it take for me to do this with joy?"*

- When I find myself spiraling downward emotionally in a state of worry and fearful about what could happen in a particular situation: *"What is the best that could happen?"*

- When I feel disempowered and helpless in a situation: *"What is the one thing I could do right now that would help?"*

- When I am going through a difficult experience or period in my life that seems to have no reason or rationale: *"How can I learn from and use this experience to contribute to and help others?"*

- When I feel like nothing is going right in my life: *"What is going right in my life right now?"* or *"What could I do right now that would help improve things?"*, and *"What are five things I could be grateful for right now?"*

Questions are powerful because they help build and sustain a framework for shifting in positive and helpful ways. They create a door...a window...or sometimes just a crack. They have the power to create an opening for a new way of thinking, for a new paradigm.

Chapter 22

Play

"Men do not quit playing because they grow old; they grow old because they quit playing." Oliver
Wendell Holmes Jr.

*"We are never more fully alive, more completely ourselves, or more deeply engrossed in anything, than
when we are at play."* Charles E. Schaefer

The value of play, except that which is competitive in nature, is minimized in our culture. Play is often considered unproductive and generally indicative of childishness and immaturity. Play is deemed appropriate and necessary for children, but adults are expected to 'grow out of it'. Play is just as essential for adults as it is for children. The expression of play may change with age, but the need for it doesn't.

Play engenders a sense of joy and freedom. It fosters creativity and nurtures relationships. It's an essential aspect of emotional and mental health. Dr. Stuart Brown, founder of the National Institute for Play and author of the book "Play", spent many years studying the importance of playing. More than six thousand cases he studied revealed that play was a vital aspect of maintaining mental, emotional and relational health. Play was found to foster emotional intimacy, deepen relationships, increase vitality, strengthen the immune system and support healing. It was even found to be an important predictor of criminal behavior. Those who grew up without playing had a much greater statistical chance of becoming involved in crime. And, of course, play can help energize your life by creating a sense of fun and joy.

What does it mean to play as an adult? Brown describes play as "purposeless, fun and pleasurable." The focus is on the experience rather than a specific end goal. Play can encompass art, music, reading, watching television and movies, joking, daydreaming, teasing, games, and more. What constitutes play and fun for one person may not be enjoyable for another. I have friends who enjoy knitting, roller coasters and swimming. I don't care for any of those things. I love to read, hike, walk on the beach and play board games with my family. I love watching the look of triumph in my husband's eyes when he makes a spectacular play during a game and his ridiculous use of hyperbole when he misses something!

I didn't grow up completely void of play, but it was often tempered by fear. My sisters and I played with our Barbie dolls a lot. We also played outside – running, building forts, playing freeze tag and hide-and-go-seek. When we were around adults, however, we quickly learned to reign in our playfulness and tread lightly. As an adult I have recognized my need to incorporate more play in my life. I'm still learning.

How can you start developing and nurturing a greater sense of play and fun in your life? It has to be intentional. Some ways to foster a greater sense of fun and play include:

- Reading or watching a short video everyday of something humorous. The internet is a great source, as well as comic books. Keeping materials that in your bathroom can be an easy way to get a steady dose of humor in your life.

- When some difficult situation arises ask yourself the question, "What is really funny about this that I am missing?" Finding the humor in a situation enables you to enter into a more comfortable relationship with the circumstances.

- Watching children play. Even better - joining them!

- Taking the risk of saying some of the funny things that you think. This may feel scary at first. It means risking sounding stupid or being misunderstood.

- Surround yourself with people who know how to play. Play, like laughter, is contagious.

- Participate in some play that does not involve competition. Have times when you are not invested in winning or losing, but simply focused on being in the moment and having unabashed fun.

- Schedule time to play and have fun in your life. Play is an important part of a balanced life. Without play life becomes drab and boring. When you lead a busy life it's easy for fun things to be relegated to a less important status.

- Join a group. There are groups for people who play cards, board games, volleyball, basketball, bingo, etc. If you are musically talented, join a choir or a band. If you are artistic take – or teach – a class. If you love to dance find a class or go to a dance club.

- Start planning for some of the fun things you have wanted to do, but haven't yet gotten around to. Some may be simple, while some may require more resources and planning.

It's important to identify and incorporate into your life the things you love to do. You deserve to enjoy your life. Taking the time to play can help bring needed balance to a fast-paced, busy life. It can prevent burnout and get you back in touch with the joy of just being alive.

Epilogue

"A diamond is merely a lump of coal that did well under the pressure" Anonymous

"Rivers know this: there is no hurry. We shall get there some day." A.A. Milne, Winnie-the-Pooh

Personal alchemy will happen all at once, and over time. There will be times when you may feel like you haven't made any progress at all. Those times are similar to what happens when walking up switchbacks on a mountain trail. Sometimes you come around the curve on the trail to encounter the same view you have seen many times before. It can be tempting to think that you aren't making any progress, because it all looks the same. There may be times when you find yourself feeling frustrated because it feels like you are back to square one. But each time you come back around to that familiar scene, you are actually a bit further up the mountain. You have the opportunity of releasing and healing residual issues from a higher perspective and accumulated wisdom.

I recently had an older patient who is experiencing tremendous emotional pain say to me, "I really want to make a shift in my life, I just feel like there's no way I have enough time to let go of everything, or make the changes I want to make." I suggested, "Just start. And consider beginning your journey with self-compassion and self-acceptance. So much of the rest is detail."

The strategies I have shared with you in this book have supported me in my work of healing – physically, mentally, emotionally and spiritually. They have been powerful tools in the alchemic process of turning my emotional lead into gold. I'm not going to pretend it has always been easy, but it has always been worth it. I'm grateful for the positive changes and lessons learned in my life so far. I feel profoundly blessed to have been able to share my heart with you in this book. Thank you for meeting me at this crossroad.

Footnotes

[1] Pert, Candice, PhD. *Molecules Of Emotion: The Science Behind Mind-Body Medicine.* Touchtone Publisher. 1997

[2] Greene, Brian. *The Elegant Universe: Superstrings, Hidden Dimensions, and the Quest for the Ultimate Theory.* New York: Vintage Books. pp.5,15-16. 2003.

[3] Doidge, Norman. *The Brain That Changes Itself: Stories of Personal Triumph from the Frontiers of Brain Science.* Penguin Books. 2007

[4] Vinoth K. Ranganathan; Vlodek Siemionowa; Jing Z. Liu; Vinod Sahgal; Guang H. Yue, "From mental power to muscle power; gaining strength by using the mind". Neuropsychologia 42. 2004.

[5] Wiseman, Richard. Lister, Ralph. *The As If Principle: The Radically New Approach To Changing Your Life.* Free Press. 2012

[6] U.S. Department of Health and Human Services. National Institute of Health; National Center for Complimentary and Alternative Medicine. http://nccam.nih.gov/health/meditation

[7] Emmons, R. A., & McCullough, M. E. "Counting blessings versus burdens: An experimental investigation of gratitude and subjective well-being in daily life". *Journal of Personality and Social Psychology.* 84(2), 377-389, 2003

[8] Emmons, Robert A. *Thanks! How Practicing Gratitude Can Make You Happier.* First Houghlin Mifflin Publishing. 2003

[9] Mendius, Richard. *Buddha's Brain: The Practical Neuroscience of Happiness, Love, and Wisdom.* New Harbinger Publications, Inc. 2009

[10] Francois Lesperance; Nancy Frasure-Smith, Etal. "The Efficacy of Omega-3 Supplementation for Major Depression: A Randomized Controlled Trial". *Journal of Clinical Psychiatry.* 2010

[11] Andrew J. Vickers, DPhil; Angel M. Cronin, MS; Alexandra C. Maschino, Etal. "Acupuncture for Chronic Pain: Individual Patient Data

Meta-analysis" *Arch Intern Med.* 2012;172(19):1444-1453.
doi:10.1001/archinternmed.2012.3654.

[12] Errington-Evans, N. "Acupuncture for anxiety". *CNS Neuroscience and Therapeutics.* 18(4), 277-284. doi: 10.1111/j.1755-5949.2011.00254.x, 2011

Additional Recommended Reading

Books:

Amen, Daniel G. *Change Your Brain, Change Your Life.* Three Rivers Press. 1998

Beinfield, Harriet, L.Ac. and Korngold, Efrem, L.Ac., O.M.D. *Between Heaven and Earth: A Guide to Chinese Medicine.* The Random House Publishing Group. 1991

Braden, Gregg. *The Spontaneous Healing of Belief.* Hay House, Inc. 2008

Brown, Brene. *The Gifts of Imperfection: Let Go of Who You Think You're Supposed to Be and Embrace Who You Are.* Hazelden. 2010

Brown, Stuart, MD and Vaughn, Christopher. *Play: How it Shapes the Brain, Opens the Imagination, and Invigorates the Soul.* The Penguin Group. 2009

Chopra, Deepak. *Quantum Healing: Exploring The Frontiers Of Mind/Body Medicine.* Bantam Books. 1989

Church, Dawson. *The Genie in Your Genes: Epigenetic Medicine and the New Biology of Intention.* Energy Psychology Press. 2009

Craig, Gary. *The EFT Manual.* Energy Psychology Press. 2008

Dawson, Karl and Allenby, Sasha, *Matrix Reimprinting Using EFT: Rewrite Your Past, Transform Your Future.* Hay House. 2010

Doidge, Norman. *The Brain That Changes Itself: Stories of Personal Triumph from the Frontiers of Brain Science.* Penguin Books. 2007

Dyer, Wayne. *There's A Spiritual Solution To Every Problem.* HarperCollins Publishers. 2001.

Emmons, Henry, and Rachel Kranz. *The Chemistry of Joy: A Three-Step Program for Overcoming Depression through Western Science and Eastern Wisdom.* New York: Simon & Schuster. 2006.

Emmons, Robert A. *Thanks! How Practicing Gratitude Can Make You Happier.* First Houghlin Mifflin Publishing. 2003

Gach, Michael Reed; Henning, Beth Ann. *Acupressure for Emotional Healing: A Self-Care Guide for Trauma, Stress, & Common Emotional Imbalances.* Bantam Book Publishing. 2004

Goertzel, Victor, Goertzel, Mildred, Goertze, Ted and Hansen, Ariel M.W. *Cradles of Eminence.* Great Potential Press. 2004

Greene, Brian. *The Elegant Universe: Superstrings, Hidden Dimensions, and the Quest for the Ultimate Theory.* Vintage Books. 2003

Gross, Jonathan. *The Great Doubt: Spirituality Beyond Dogma.* CreateSpace. 2010

Hanh, Tich Nhat. *Peace Is Every Step.* Bantam Books. 1991

Harden, Blaine. *Escape From Camp 14: One Man's Remarkable Odyssey from North Korea to Freedom in the West.* The Penguin Group. 2012

Hawkins, David. *Power vs. Force.* Hay House.1995

Hoobyar, Tom; Dotz, Tom; Sanders, Susan. *NLP: The Essential Guide to Neuro-Linguistic Programming.* HarperCollins Books. 2013

Jampolsky, Gerald, G. *Forgiveness: The Greatest Healer of All.* Beyond Words Publishing Inc. 1999

Katie, Byron. *I Need Your Love – Is That True?.* Harmony Books. 2005

Keith, Kent, M. *Anyway: The Paradoxical Commandments.* G.P. Putnam's Sons. 2001

Lambrou, Charles. *The Alchemist's Way* (E-book). 2011

Lambrou, Peter, T; Pratt, George. *Instant Emotional Healing: Acupressure for the Emotions*. Broadway Books. 2006

Levine, Peter, A; Gabor, Mate. *In an Unspoken Voice: How the Body Releases Trauma and Restores Goodness*. North Atlantic Books, 2010

Lipton, Bruce H. *The Biology of Belief*. Hay House. 2005

Mathews, Andrea. *The Law of Attraction: The Soul's Answer to Why It Isn't Working and How It Can*. O-Books. 2011

McTaggart, Lynne. *The Field*. HarperCollins Publishing. 2002

Mendius, Richard. *Buddha's Brain: The Practical Neuroscience of Happiness, Love, and Wisdom*. New Harbinger Publications, Inc. 2009

Nelson, Bradley. *The Emotion Code*. Wellness Unmasked Publishing. 2007

Pearsall, Paul. *The Beethoven Factor: The New Positive Psychology of Hardiness, Happiness, Healing, and Hope*. Hampton Roads Publishing Company, Inc. 2003

Talbot, Michael. *The Holographic Universe*. Harper Collins. 1991

Tolle, Eckhart. *The Power of Now*. Namaste Publishing. 1999

Trevino, Haven. *The Tao of Healing: Meditations for Body and Spirit*. New World Library. 1999

Zukav, Gary. *The Dancing Wu Li Masters*. Perennial Classics. 2001

Wiseman, Richard; Lister, Ralph. *The As If Principle: The Radically New Approach To Changing Your Life*. Free Press. 2012

Articles:

Emmons RA, et al. "Counting Blessings Versus Burdens: An Experimental Investigation of Gratitude and Subjective Well-Being in

Daily Life," *Journal of Personality and Social Psychology* (Feb. 2003): Vol. 84, No. 2, pp. 377–89.

Grant AM, et al. "A Little Thanks Goes a Long Way: Explaining Why Gratitude Expressions Motivate Prosocial Behavior," *Journal of Personality and Social Psychology* (June 2010): Vol. 98, No. 6, pp. 946–55.

Sansone RA, et al. "Gratitude and Well Being: The Benefits of Appreciation," *Psychiatry* (Nov. 2010): Vol. 7, No. 11, pp. 18–22.

Seligman MEP, et al. "Empirical Validation of Interventions," *American Psychologist* (July–Aug. 2005): Vol. 60, No. 1, pp. 410–21

Internet:

"Sleep loss linked to psychiatric disorders". Yasmin Anwar, Media Relations | 22 October 2007, http://berkeley.edu/news/media/releases/2007/10/22_sleeploss.shtml

Double Slit Experiment: http://www.livescience.com/19268-quantum-double-slit-experiment-largest-molecules.html

"Brain May Flush Out Toxins During Sleep". http://www.nih.gov/news/health/oct2013/ninds-17.htm, National Institute of Health, October, 2013

"Alchemy is the art of manipulating life, and consciousness in matter, to help it evolve, or to solve problems of inner disharmonies. – Jean Dubuis

Daniel Ray Photography

.

About the Author: Dr. Diane Gross is a Doctor of Oriental Medicine, a Licensed Acupuncturist and a Holistic Life Coach. She specializes in assisting people in healing from both physical and emotional pain. She teaches workshops on personal alchemy, forgiveness, stress management, vicarious trauma, strategies for releasing fear and anger and other related topics. Dr. Gross is Managing Practitioner at Stillpoint Acupuncture in Greensboro, NC, where she currently lives with her husband. She has three grown sons and two grandchildren

Please visit our website at www.theartofpersonalalchemy.com

Made in the USA
Charleston, SC
14 July 2015